A HEAD ON MY SHOULDERS

A FIRST NOVEL
by
VESPER HUNTER

Vesper Hunter

Published by

Malvern Publishing Company Limited
PO Box 16
Malvern
Worcestershire
WR14 1UH
England

ISBN 0-947993-07-X

Printed and bound in Great Britain by
Sharp Bros. (Printers) Ltd., Evesham, Worcs.

ACKNOWLEDGEMENTS

I am most grateful to R. A. Henderson of Eastbourne, who shared with me his researches into the history of the Hungerford family at Down Ampney and built up the connections between the Dunches, Hungerfords, Lisles and Beconshaws, and was an encouraging critic.

I am also grateful to Eric Cullingford, who shared his wealth of historical knowledge with generous enthusiasm, and found no detail or weighty problem beyond his concern.

There are special friends who must also be mentioned for they know that without their encouragement this diary would have been begun but never finished. I have valued so much their help and support.

I owe a great debt to the pamphlets, guides and records held in the parishes Dame Alice Lisle knew well—Ellingham, Dibden, Crux, Easton, Chilton Foliat, Wootton, Isle of Wight and many others. Tombs, inscriptions and monuments have revealed many secrets. Records offices and Archivists are always helpful, and the librarians at Malvern Library have been patient and unflagging in their help.

INTRODUCTION

Three hundred years ago Dame Alice Lisle lived in Moyles Court, a gracious house near Ringwood, in Hampshire. Three hundred years later. I also found that I shared her birthdate, so that, when I lived there, I was her age, and had in fact, a similar matriarchal position in the household as she had had before me. That is not all, and I must briefly recount the coincidences that brought Dame Alice Lisle very close to me, so that I can say I know her well and feel her blessing on my writing her diary for a year of her life, mid-way between the murder of her husband and her own execution in 1685.

Moyles Court, this great house on the edge of the New Forest, was in a cold, sad state of neglect and decay when I saw it first in deep snow and frost with bitter draughts and icy winds piercing through broken windows and cobwebbed panelling. It was for sale—with "Vacant Possession", the board said, but was that true if a ghost was known to live there? She had been seen in living memory, "on the panelled landing", "in the minstrels' gallery", "by the big gates". Poor Dame Alice! She had been torn away from that house to her execution in Winchester in 1685, condemned for treason by Judge Jeffreys, for harbouring refugees from the battle of Sedgemoor, in her home. Lawyers and historians agree that the verdict was correct. An American lady wrote to me soon after we moved in to ask my permission to publish the story of the saffron-robed figure who passed her and disappeared round the corner of the landing as she sat by the window one day in the empty house. She had had no idea of any "haunted" story, nor that they said that a coach and horses could be heard galloping down Ellingham Drove on windy nights, towards Winchester.

When Southern Television came to film Moyles Court soon

7

after we moved in, trying to flog up public interest and concern for young children living in a haunted house, Lucy, aged ten, when asked what she felt about it, said, "We don't mind! She is a kind old lady and I think she likes to watch us playing and being happy, but we don't talk about it in front of the little ones." Lucy was right and her awareness of Dame Alice had an authenticity from her own experience as valid as the researches of historians or lawyers into the ghost-figures that others saw.

We who lived there never saw her, but I, for one, became very aware of her. Neither demolition nor new building nor the 300 years that separated us could keep us apart. So many things drew us together but in 1974 my experiences were especially close to Dame Alice's of 1674. People ask if I feel I am a reincarnation of her. I am not. She is a close and kindred spirit. They ask if I have seen her. I do not think I am temperamentally the sort of person to "see" a spirit.

But I do know her.

They ask if I make up the events in her diary. I can only say that they happen. I have checked and cross-checked the historical facts, but the diary is an imaginative reconstruction which is convincing to me as I have come closer and closer to the woman who wrote through me. Was she guilty of treason? The reader of the diary must decide. I scorn the thought. Historians and lawyers must judge from their evidence, but I share the feelings and concerns of a warm, thinking, sensitive human person. Centuries do not alter these things.

No execution, no human judgement, no passing of time, can destroy the spirit she left in the home where she lived when she had, "a head on her shoulders", and it is on her behalf that I have written her diary.

Asterisks in the text refer
to notes at the back of the
book under the relevant dates.

"A HEAD ON MY SHOULDERS"

Alice Lisle's Diary—1674

JANUARY

Tuesday 1st January

A New year begins to-day and for me a new decade, I shall be sixty this year and it is ten years since Sir John was killed in Lausanne. As I heard the ringers last night ringing in the New Year and the household had gone to bed, I sat over the dying embers of the Hall fire (new iron grate and basket from the Gorley forge a *great* success)* I mused over my more than half century of life. Turbulent, political unrest, civil war, three kings and a Commonwealth, amazing discoveries in science, a great wealth of new knowledge and learning, a daughter in a new world discovered and colonised over the ocean, but— for me it has been the forging of my own faith—now as firm and strong as my new fire-grate!—that has been my life. The estrangement from my husband*, the little community of people I lead here and who join me in our private and semi-secret happenings on Sundays*, the sad and hopeless rejection of me by, and my own hostility towards, the churches in Ellingham and at Ibsley and now Fordingbridge too (and of course Ringwood)—these are the springs of my life and the source of strength to my spirit. Just now it is John Hicks, who means more to me than any man alive.

Wednesday 2nd January

Puzzled all day by John Hicks's message. What does he mean? What does he know of my *needs*? I need his support and understanding and acceptance. I desperately need the understanding of a sincere person and John means so much to me. I love him for his insight into himself, the ease with which he has unburdened his searchings and heartache to me. "I cannot meet your needs." I wandered down to the ford and crossed the footbridge, for the Dockens is full, with snow melting from Fritham and the heath. Walked alongside the stream and saw wild deer and a squirrel rooting for acorns among the sodden leaves and trees scored by his tusk. How destructive they are. Must send the men out tomorrow to get him. What does John mean? The priest in him has not wholly masked the man, and I love the man behind his role, though a generation separates us.

Back in the evening as dark fell and heard Harriet with the madrigal singers as I came past the chapel. Called in to the servants' hall and listened. They have a new one—"Flora gave me fairest flowers" brought down from Derbyshire, that gave spring thought to this wintry day. Little James Mist brought me the first aconite*.

Thursday 3rd January

A strange feeling all day that I am part of all history, all philosophy, all knowledge— a sort of heart of everything. I have glimpses of and feeling for what the Catholics hold to, what Presbyterians, Puritans, Calvinists, Royalists, Parliamentarians "see". I stand at the centre and "see" it all. I *cannot* belong to *any* 'party'. I 'touch' the ancient classical world. I reverence the mystery of those around me who study these multifarious new sciences, astrology, astronomy, mathematics, the world of medical research, the mystery of the circulation of blood, the movement of earth and stars and sun. I am a child of the renaissance and of new learning. I am the voyager to this new world beyond our seas. I support the King. I fight for Commonwealth. It all comes from my love of my God, and I am in and with Him at the heart of it all— neither humanly knowing or understanding anything, but spiritually at one with it all. These thoughts came clear as I held James's aconite yesterday and heard the singers. Is it beauty or truth that is really at the heart of life? Or is it most surely seen in the *way* we live? Snow fell to-night with darkness and Harriet helped me with the damask. (She is learning lace-making!! An "idle woman's pastime" they say!—But it is skilful and dexterous and lovely. I *would* approve!)

Friday 4th January

A white world. Much shovelling of snow by everyone and the

children sliding down the Cuckoo pines and Whitefield and the woodpile buried deep and the wood brought in damp and steaming. Ben brought hot ale down to the ford as a wheel came off a cart from Gorley Farm in the middle of the snow and broken ice and they had a job to get it out. Their old horse was panicky and stumbling and shivering and sweating and splashing water and ice over everyone. Bitterly cold. I hope this isn't the start of a 1620 winter. I remember that, and I was only six!—I remember a great fear that it would *never* be warm again. Snow fell hard in April that year and lay until May, my father said—or was that the year I was born?! The Thames was frozen over, for *that* we heard when Parliament was recalled and folk had to travel up and down to London and Winchester and news travelled fast, for the Montagu children came to stay and taught me to skate on Fritham pond! (Or did they skate and I merely slid!?) Strange muddled childish recollections. Much clear in the confusion and this year brings it back.

Saturday 5th January

Slipped last night on the ice and my wrist very painful to-day. Harriet fussing with hot and cold compresses and herbs so I make light of it to allay her anxiety! Dear faithful Harriet! What a good friend she has been since Sir John fled to Lausanne and I carried the responsibility for the welfare of the Moyles Court lands alone, and the Beconshaw property since my father died. I love it all and the people of the Forest, too. They have become my life and my purpose.

Sunday 6th January

Walked to Ellingham church through the snow with Harriet Mist and Margaret who had driven over from Fordingbridge as Robert* had gone to Winchester for Epiphany. Snow melting, trees dripping and the whole sodden wood reflected my mood. It is no good, I can find *no* sincerity or reality in the Mass any more. The notion that the bread and wine is changed to body and flesh is too close to the wizardry and alchemy that the church so quickly condemns. (Margaret says they caught a witch in Fordingbridge last week and ducked her in the river). I can bear *none* of this, and only went to Ellingham Church this morning to set some sort of example in

11

the Moyles Court pew of loyalty to Christ, for the sake of the simple folk on the estate. But I am only pushing falsehood and sham at them, and I watched their faces, some bored, some eager and expectant, some pompous and arrogant. Margaret, by my side, was devout and detached—she has accepted Robert's discipline!—But never really thinks for herself. I wish I had her willing obedience and conforming nature. The group came out from Ringwood in the evening. Marvellous free understanding between us. They understand my impossible position. My *own* seeing is the only reality to me and I will *not* accept a sham.

Monday 7th January

Parliament is recalled to-day. I know because Lord Shaftesbury (made Chancellor nearly two years ago and lost office last November) went through Ringwood from Wimborne St. Giles on Saturday. His ostler's boy came to see my stable boy James Dunne, the new one from Horton*) briefly on Saturday night, Harriet told me. Oh. politics and religion! "The letter killeth and the spirit giveth life." The Lords and Commons will press the King to give freedom to Protestants, and it will all be decided by the King. I cannot bear it. Out Lord fought against this and I will fight the same fight—for the life of spirit—the life of my spirit. I will not be bound by clergy or minister, by King or Bishop, by this prayer book or that ordinance, by Catholic or Presbyterian or Protestant or Anglican, or even the new Quakers. I will be *free*—not beyond learning and beyond law, but believing most deeply that I am a child of God, and through faith in Jesus as the Christ (not as 'God') I will have faith in and be obedient to what he reveals in and to the Christian me, daily, hourly, every moment. I am learning much of loving through my love for John Hicks. How can I learn from or be kept true by Bishops and Lords kneeling to the King and buying their position and structure from him in Laws and Decrees? In my life-time the world's struggle to cage the spirit has been endless. I see the priests' with butterfly nets trying to harness God to do their will and I will have none of it.

Tuesday 8th January

> Roll back the night and let the grey dawn break,
> Wake to the sodden winter wet and wind
> To misty hills and gaunt cold-fingered trees
> Which every morning etch the coming dawn.
> A blackbird sings, incredibly bright
> For this December morning, with the leaves
> Rotting and shining on the compost bed
> And Christmas carcase bleaching on the rose.
> Light grows!—Light grows each winter dawn
> With promise always of a brave new day.
> Maybe the aconite this morning bursts,
> Pushing with greeny elbow, through the soil,
> Cradling its earliest flower—a golden pearl.
> In any winter dawn at just this hour
> Of daybreak, these things come to be.
> Let there be light then—and there was the Light!
> Each dawn, new hope! Each dawn a new years's day.
> (Or—And faith and hope and love again—these three)

Harriet rescued the scrap of paper on which I scribbled this, from my apron pocket in the laundry! I wrote it on New Year's Eve. There's been little laundry done since Christmas, what with madrigals and mummers and the snow. No sign of John H.

Wednesday 9th January

In these dark cold days my plans go ahead for the building of the new wing to the house. With the group coming out regularly from, not only Ringwood village now, but from Horton and Holt and the Forest and meeting faithfully in the chapel, I know we need each other and the wing could be used as hostelry, or for over-night stays for those who want to share with us our simple, basic study of the Gospels and our getting to know our God—uncluttered by sermons and treatises and clouds of incense and various prayer-books, accepted, rejected, reformed, renewed. They are all escapes from the simple demands of Jesus. Has the Reformation really made any difference for us? The Bible was totally hidden by a foreign tongue and the secret club of the priesthood and the dead symbols that had been meaningful in the Middle Ages had lost their message. But now? The Reformation broke the old shell, but the confusion now, the multiplicity of sects and schisms, of interpretations and translations, the confusions of scholars and theologians, has hidden the truth as surely as it was hidden before. The Restoration of the Monarchy has simplified nothing and the Court wears its church label and then defies its Lord, holding no standards but the love of self, and the lust for power and wealth.

Thursday 10th January

Slow thaw all day and the trees dripping and the ground sodden and the ford flooded, with ice still at the edges. I went out to pick the first periwinkle but have a streaming cold and decided to come back in—Harriet and Susan giving me peppermint tea and balsam inhalation!—by the fire. No John Hicks. Is he held up by the weather? I thought of him so much to-day and my strange and deep feeling for him. His mind is alive and free, but his priesthood binds him in fetters. He is still young, only 40, could be my son! Why do I pin so much faith and hope in him and see in him the Christ in England today. (But Jesus threw aside the priesthood and politics and the bindings of the law, and fulfilled all these things in his Father's love for him.) If I was known to harbour thoughts like this (about J.H.) I would be labelled a blasphemous heretic by the church, against the King, and a law-breaking infidel. How hard it is in England to-day to think freely and yet never before has such freedom of thought been about—in sect or party, in poetry, philosophy or art.

Friday 11th January

A wild boar came down from the Forest to-day and gored old Smithers at the top of Ibsley Drove. He was lying on the ground, having fallen over a tree trunk buried in the snow and would soon have been savaged to death but for Will Stacey's deerhounds which must have been on the boar's scent for they drove it off; and Will, hearing them calling, came and found Smithers bleeding profusely in the thigh. They carried him up here on an old door just at dusk this evening and we will keep him here till morning. The gash is deep and he has lost much blood and is moaning in pain. His daughter from Gorley came later and will stay with her father, so I sent Susan down to look after her children till tomorrow. Her husband, (Herbert the Charcoal burner), will not be home till late tomorrow night. Though Henry is fifteen and a sensible boy she was worried about the younger ones. Smithers delirious and in great pain.

Saturday 12th January

Betty Smithers called me before daybreak to help her with her father who had tossed restlessly all night. Sent James Dunne at daybreak to bring back the apothecary with herbs for sleep and healing and they returned by mid-morning. Mr. Bolwell was kind and gentle and brewed strange concoctions in the kitchen of bark and herbs and bones and "chemicals" (he said) and some were for drink and some for bathing and some were ointments for salving and dressing the wounds. I watched and assisted and was puzzled and suspicious, wondering how much was done to give him power over us and how much had genuine healing property. The discoveries of scientific medicines and new surgical skills have hardly reached us yet down here, but I feel they will soon surpass our simple ways. Yet I feel, and felt as I watched Mr. Bolwell, that the healings of our Lord were both simpler and more profound for they healed the heart and touched the spirit where God is. (What am I writing! This thought would be seen as blasphemy by any priest! Not J.H.?)

Sunday 13th January

The epistle read together in Moyles Court chapel to-day was deeply moving for us all:—"Everything will soon come to an end, so, to pray better, keep a calm and sober mind. Above all, never let your love for each other grow insincere, since love cancels innumerable sins. Welcome each other into your houses ungrudgingly. Each one of you has received a special grace, so, like good stewards, responsible for all these different graces of God, put yourselves at the service of others. If you are a speaker, speak as if you uttered words from God; if you are a helper, help as though every action were done at God's orders, so that in everything God may receive the glory, through Jesus Christ, since to him alone belong all glory and power for ever and ever. Amen".

My thoughts flew from this to the new wing*. It must be my service to our group, for the love of God.

Betty took her father back home as she felt the family would need her and her husband will be back. Sent them down in the cart. Smithers calmer now and the pain eased but it is a nasty wound.

Monday 14th January

A messenger from Winchester came at lunch-time with a message from John Hicks*. He will be here on Saturday night and wants us to meet on Sunday in our room here. He must leave for Lyme by noon and is sailing from there to France, (Why?) and does not want his coming known to any one other than our group. My heart sang and I spent the day going here and there adjusting these rushes and sweeping that corner and—far too soon!—being ready for his coming. I did not know the messenger, who accepted mead and cheese and bread and venison pasty, and then galloped off towards Salisbury with no mention of his destination.

Tuesday 15 January

Puzzled much of the day over Rev. John Hicks. He says so little, and only in rare outbursts has he unburdened his thoughts to me. He finds it hard to see the function of a priest in this present world, for, though he has more learning than the common folk, he said once to me, "I learn more from the simple cottager and the village children, now that they can hear the Gospel in their own language, than from the theologians and scholars who wrangle and wrestle for the truth. Their seeing is direct and simple and untroubled".

Wednesday 16th January

Slow moving days, though the evenings are lengthening a little. Frost has returned and the puddles are covered with ice and the streams brittle and the children sucking the pieces! I scolded them at the ford to-day and took them back to give them icicles from the coach-house pump. Harriet's little James is always up to mischief. I hope her care for me does not make her neglect her duty as a mother. I must warn her for he is running wild. But the week is going slowly as I long for Saturday and John's return.

Thursday 17th January

Another frosty night and the sun rose crimson over the forest
and deer moved through the mist down to the stream. How
far away the years in London seem, for my heart is in the
country, though when I was younger I thrilled to the noise and
bustle of the town. A very puritan streak has developed in me
in the last years. More so, strangely, since the end of the
Commonwealth and John's murder. I would have expected to
have sympathised with Cromwell and Sir John's total
disapproval of the lavish display and luxury of Court and
Church, but I found their attitude so hard and hostile and
critical. Not till after the Restoration did I myself come to
despise ostentatious display, the power of the church and the
haughty superiority of the Court. Had Oliver Cromwell lived
and the Commonwealth survived and Sir John held power
would I have been a different sort of person?

Friday 18th January

Spent the day longing for tomorrow. Made pasties and pies in
the morning. The men had brought in rabbits and pheasant
and a hare from shooting in the copse beyond the deer park
this morning. It will help with the food on Sunday.

John arrived just after dark. A day sooner than he said.

Saturday 19th January

I'm writing this over the fire full of sizzling damp oak logs for
gales have been blowing most of this week and many trees
have fallen, and the timber pile is soaked.

It must have been two hours after darkness fell that I heard
voices raised and horses' feet in the yard and hurried out and
John Hicks had arrived. He was drenched and mud-soaked
and his man-servant bore him off to tend him. An hour (or
eternity!) later he came in to the library—clean and smiling
and embraced me. They brought us food and ale and Harriet
waited on us with as much care and concern as I would have
done, but I longed for them to go and leave us in peace. At last
they did so and we were alone. But John seemed withdrawn
and never mentioned where he was going in France. He is
deeply distressed at the death of one of his closest friends
there—(That may be why he is going over?)—a man called

Drury with whom he has lived in Paris and a free-thinker, as he is,—one time Calvinist. John was so tired, reserved and sad so I retired early for his sake and left him free to sleep, for he must leave tomorrow. That's why he came a day early.

Sunday 20th January

Long before daylight I heard the group arriving from Ringwood—James Bolwell apothecary, and Mary Steele and son, the Brown sisters, riding behind old man Day and Mrs. Hiscock from Ibsley with her daughter and son-in-law. Then there was our own household—seventeen of us altogether. John moved us deeply, preaching about our closeness to death and our need to be ready to move to fuller life beyond this. He quoted from William Penn: "They that love beyond the world cannot be separated by it. Death cannot kill that which never dies. Nor can spirits ever be divided, that love and live in the same divine principle, the root and record of their friendship. If absence be not death, neither is theirs. Death is but crossing the world as friends do the seas; they live in one another still. This is the comfort of friends that though they may be said to die, yet their friendship and society are, in the best sense, ever-present, because immortal." I alone knew of the death of the man Drury in Paris for whom he grieved. John left just before dusk. Later than he intended. As he held me to say good bye he said, "I'm going to France in the morning, but I will be back. Don't let this be known", and he was gone.

Monday 21st January

Yesterday seems a dream. He has gone again. And late in the morning Betty Smithers came in tears, for her father died in the night. The shock of the wound was too much and it was deeply poisoned, and Betty grieved for she had felt helpless. So the day was full of preparations for the funeral at Harbridge on Wednesday. And just yesterday John had made us all think of death. He quoted Bp. John Pearson of Chester on the communion of Saints—"The saints on earth share with angels and saints in heaven. Such persons as are truly sanctified while they live among the crooked generations of men and struggle with the miseries of this world, have fellowship with the angels, and with the saints who have departed.

18

Nor is this communion separated by the death of any since Christ is he in whom they live and their fellowship is with the saints who now enjoy the presence of the Father." How close to living these truths we must be in these days with old Smithers gone, and John's friend, Drury, in Paris, and John yesterday turning our thoughts to death, and Civil War vivid in our memory and the execution of a King and plagues and fires all very recent happenings.

Tuesday 22nd January

Spent the day at Gorley with Harriet helping Betty prepare for tomorrow's funeral. The children looked bewildered and sad, though Harry gallantly played the man to his mother.

Wednesday 23rd January

The funeral to-day of Dick Smithers. All the village and Moyles Court folk were there. No time to write to-day. My time has been spent at Harbridge church with the mourners.

Thursday 24th January

Brought in snowdrops, periwinkle and aconites from the woods in Ellingham Drove, not knowing what I was to find on my return. Met a bewildered, angry, grief-stricken Harriet with a tearful story of the theft of linen from my oak chest. She had finished laundering and went to get fresh sheets, only to find the best ones, with old Grandma Beconshaw's hand-made lace (must be a hundred years old at least) gone, and the lavender and rosemary strewn all over the drawers. She says she feels sure it was taken by two servants of Col. Penruddock's* at Hale. He had turned them out for thieving from him and they had spent a day and a night in the stocks at Wood Green. They then turned up here and helped with the dragging in of timber from the Forest and had been hanging about here for several days, for the story of their thieving ways had not reached us. They were hefty louts—all brawn and no brain and disappeared on Monday towards Martin through the forest. We have no evidence that it was them so can do little about it. Poor Harriet! I could not scold *her*!

Friday 25th January

Harriet still tearful. Barter* & Dowding, the two suspected thieves of my linen, have left many stories behind of cunning and pilfering, and the army and police and bailifs have been alerted. I dare not send a message to Col. Penruddock although, as the local magistrate, he should be the one to be told. We have not been on friendly terms since Sir John had his 'serious disagreement' with that household and I prefer to let my linen go rather than contact him.

I should go to London tomorrow but have sent a message to Fritham House to tell them that domestic circumstances force me to stay at home. The police may well return for detailed enquiries and Harriet, in her anxiety, will confuse things. (The only lace of Grandma Beconshaw's that is now left at Moyles Court is the small edging I gave Harriet last Christmas that she stitched to her pinafore.*) Bridget and Margaret and Tryfona had all the rest in their wedding dowries. I have none!

Sunday 27th January

Meeting was very thin this morning. I had expected to be in London so had not arranged for a chaplain, and this news had spread to Ringwood and Linford. The forester came from Linwood and four from Ibsley and Betty Smithers came. I led them mostly in silence—and there was peace. Afterwards I went to church at Ellingham with most of the household. Took James Dunne in the carriage with me, for he still feels strange among us and has much teasing to bear from the younger men and I wanted to spare him the walk down the drove. I told him I needed someone to help me from the carriage to the church door, up that muddy, slippery path! (Partly true!) Felt rebellious in church. Not an uncommon feeling. The Vicar was coldly polite. He finds me difficult and distrusts me for I never give him the obsequious respect he wants. He is a worldly man and I think, a secret drinker.

FEBRUARY

Friday 1st February

January over and a week with nothing to note in this journal.
Wet and cold and flood and short dark days, and I have kept
indoors. The police have no news of Barter and Dowding. It
is so easy for thieves and ne'er-do-wells to cross a county
boundary into Dorset or Wiltshire from here and so escape. I
shall not see that linen again—nor the men!

I'm writing this by one single candle light (in the tall holder
I love!) Candles are so condemned as part of popery. I laugh
at heart at this innocent little candle flame as it splutters and
struggles and then burns again steadily, and then wavers in
any tiny draught! Popery?! You can make anything a symbol
of your love or hate and I will accept everything, not as
symbolic but as sacramental, and my little candle is the Light
of the World, a fragment of the great Sun, and I just—love
candlelight!—I love the candles burning in the churches, and
cannot dismiss them as being the hypocrisy and sham I shun.
That is in men—not light. No one really understands me.
(J.H. does).

Saturday 2nd February

Slept badly and was wide awake long before dawn. Sat at my
window. Prayed? But not in words, for neither prayer book
nor priestly words, not any spoken sound brings me close to
my God. They make a barrier, just as the carved oak screen at
Ellingham makes patterned darkness between me and the
light of the holy places. Dawn broke and I watched the deer
grazing through the mist, lifting great antlers against the
opening day. Light again. Not my little guttering candle,
which now hung a waxy head by my side, but the quiet,
silently moving, growing coming of the day. Light growing
out of darkness. Hardly at first seen to be light, so dim and
faint it is, and yet—the harbinger of the true Light which

lighteth every man that cometh into the world. My prayers were neither words nor even thought, but there was within me and without, an awareness, an at-one-ness—all light was the true Light; all life was the Life of the world. All belief, all unbelief was one with Truth and so day (and light) broke again—and I had a busy day getting kitchens and hall ready for a Mr. White, who came before dark with his company from Winchester, to lead our meeting tomorrow.

Sunday 3rd February

Our meeting was packed, and when it was over I moved amongst them in a trance having been deeply affected by words used by our preacher. (A dull, sombre, sad and solemn man, yet what he said has moved me deeply.) He read some words from a young Hereford writer, now chaplain to the Bridgmans at Teddington (whom I met a few years ago), Thomas Traherne:

"Your person is the greatest gift your Love can offer up to God Almighty. Clothe yourself with Light as with a garment when you come before Him: put on the greatness of Heaven and Earth . . . Be all the knowledge and light you are able, as great, as clear, as perfect as possible. So at length you shall appear before God and as God converse with God for evermore."

And the faces of the meeting were solemn and unmoved as if nothing special had been said. And solemn, sad Mr. White, said those words, and seemed unfired by them. And I?—I felt uplifted and powerful and full of insight and also humbled and cast down and insignificant. At last they all left, and the party from Winchester left to journey to Breamore for the night and—I was left to consider all I had heard.

Monday 4th February

How do I write about to-day? I'm in my room, having pretended to Harriet that I must sleep. She has gone down to the kitchens and it must be after seven o'clock, but I must have time alone, though I am in tears and tired and torn and shaken. My candle gutters and my hand shakes and tears fall. Yesterday's meeting moved me deeply, and I clung to those words of Traherne's which were not words but a truth I knew from my heart. The morning was foggy and the forest hidden; there was noise everywhere since no one wanted to get out to work. I knew I must be alone, and slipped out in the fog to the ford and then alongside the Dockens Water and I was lost in thought, forgot time, and—how long later?—was not by the stream, but in the fog surrounded by bog and gorse and myrtle and heather and sinking, with no idea of direction. Then I slipped and was up to my waist in mud and thorn and sphagnum and I was frightened and the fog thick, and I—lost. Time became eternity; and life, death, and space, became the point where I was, alone, and, deep in my fear. Then came the words "Clothe yourself with light . . . and as God converse with God for evermore." I died in that bog and then was alive again.

I found strength and floundered on and on to the higher ground and then, miracle, the Fritham track and so, home, to Harriet fussing, and now—I'm alone again.

Tuesday 5th February

Fog thicker than ever, and Harriet giving me milk and honey and mint tea and camomile and—I am miles from it all. "Delirious!" I heard her say, but, no, though I am glad to be up in my room all day, for what has happened to me since Sunday's meeting is of a depth I have not known before—unearthly, heavenly, real, eternal. "As God converse with God for evermore." I have found a faith within myself in the God within, at one with the God without, and I know the Above to be one with the Below, and if we would stop, as I was forced to stop yesterday, in the fog and the bog, outside time and space, stripped of all knowledge and strength, alone and lost—all our frenzied wranglings, quarrels, prides and powers would fall away, and we would be conversing, God with God for evermore. I must be faithful to my inner light where God is, fuelling my tiny flame. This is not taught in Catholic or Protestant churches; this is not contained in creed or crowd, or found in the words of preacher or priest—and yet Thomas Traherne has put it into words that for me are a light in the fog, firm ground in the bog, life in death. God is within, without, above, below—I converse, God with God.

23

Wednesday 6th February

How what I write here would be condemned as blasphemy were it known. I dare share the experience of Monday with no one, except John Hicks next time he is here. Yet I must share it somehow with the Group, but carefully, gently, lest I give offence—as truth so often does.

Got up and went below again, and was eyed suspiciously by my household who had heard of my 'foolish' ways, in venturing out alone in the fog. Sent for the new side of bacon to be cut up as I knew this would reassure them all that I was well and in good humour, and we ate well in the early afternoon. I called the men in from the stable and the farm to join us and we all had mead. Much humour about, for they thought me, not only foolish, but also a little mad!—Or, at least, that is how I interpreted the way they eyed me and then shifted off or hurried away to exchange comments behind their hands or round the corners. We resalted and stored the uncut joints and I had many volunteers to take a joint down to Betty Smithers. (They were afraid I would go myself into the fog again!) And deep within me was my truth, first lighted by Mr. Traherne and then made one with me in the helplessness and fear, nearly sucked into bog, and unseeing and lost in fog—and then the inner light.

Thursday, 7th February

I have stored last Monday's episode deep in my mind. It will be part of me for ever—one of lifes milestones, pointers, clearings on my journey, like the tumps and cairns that mark the forest tracks. The fog has cleared, and it is sodden and wet. A cart called by from London—one of Lord Shaftesbury's returning home with goods he had bought and he was afraid they would be vandalised unless he got them away. He sent a group of twelve of his men, six on horse, and the others on the cart as there are robbers everywhere. (He has promised his men a good reward if they get to Wimborne St. Giles in safety.) Poor fellows!—They'd pressed on in the days of fog feeling that was safer than being seen on the highway, but had had a perilous time, and came by Moyles Court to have a night here with our protection.

They brought rumours, mostly gossip, about the King, swaying this way and that, trying always to placate Catholics and Protestants and in fear always of Parliament, knowing decisions must be his, and not knowing who is really friend and who foe. So—the double life—political intrigue, and the frivolity of Court. It all seems such a farce when the news seeps down to us in the Forest.

Friday 8th February

Skirmish in the morning as the Shaftesbury cart got under way, I was glad when they had gone, though the merriment here last night as they were fed and warmed and relaxed, was good for us all, and gave us a diversion from the long, wet, dark, winter days and nights. I hope they get back safely and earn their reward—not because the Shaftesburys need more wealth and riches, but because the men were decent fellows and I would like them to prove themselves honest and trustworthy, too. (Dear simple James Dunne again enjoyed his friendship with the ostler's boy! I watched them fooling together and was glad, for James has to bear so much teasing for his simple ways.)

The Shaftesbury coach brought the news of the end of the Dutch Wars. Although little of that reaches us down here I'm glad it is over, for the Dutch are our Protestant friends and I dislike the thought of us fighting against them with Catholic French as our allies. But—it all seems unreal and far away, and more the King's affair than ours!—Though he will look to us, land-owners, to pay his bills, no doubt!

Saturday 9th February

There are three dark weeks ahead, and I feel I must try to write in this journal what my views on life really are, what are my religious, political, personal views. I am confused. My life has confused me. Change has come all round, and I have known the execution of a King; frightening civil war; the break out in disunity of so many religious views', while Law and Book direct our prayer and our priests. There have been wars in Europe with confusions of intrigues, the restoration of a monarchy and unbelievable corruption at court. Then there's the New World, new scientific exploration and discovery; new literature; learning; poetry; painting. Where am I in all this? I, who have been accused of treachery, treason, nonconformity, laxity, understand well why I am suspect. Yet I know, at heart, my own simplicity and my love of small unchanging country, forest, ways, with morris dancers, ballad mongers, Fordingbridge fair and May Day revels!— And the geese flying in in the winter and first snowdrops in the woods, and my deep understanding and love for a young, confused fighting priest whom I can never really know—and deep down, my love for God.

Sunday 10th February

So—no more daily jottings, but an attempt in these coming days, to summarise what life has taught me.

News of the end of the Dutch War confirmed at evensong at Ellingham this evening.

Monday 11th February

I want to capture my views on

Politics.

Why do I choose to write about this first? Because, in spite of my distrust of all things political, and my distrust of decisions made by parties and groups, (which have always seemed to me to be swayed by the ambitions and pretences of the men who formed the group), politics have played a great part in my life, where monarchy has been deposed and civil war has taught us to distrust even those in our own households, and a Commonwealth has shaken our old ways so deeply that old times of gracious and peaceful living have gone for ever. I have known the execution of a King, appointed by Divine Law. I have known the restoration of another, whose court is so corrupt that Divine Law is made a mockery. I have known my own husband killed because of the part he played in politics. How can I hold to any one political party, one political view, when I have watched this strife and wrangling throughout my life? All it brings about is increased prices, where the King applies taxes and fells forest for his needs, and Commonwealth demands money to pay for wars at home, and overseas? It all leaves me confused and bewildered and I am glad to finish this page and write no more!

Tuesday 12th February

Yet—when I read what I wrote yesterday I know that within me I am a Royalist and will support the King. I do belive Kings are appointed under God and by Divine Right, as I believe, too, that I am appointed under God and by Divine Right to order my Moyles Court household in peace and love and security. I know, too, that I support those who would refuse to give the King power to oppress his people, to trample on the poor, tax the rich, and dictate the religion of both the learned and the ignorant. Yet, there is a sense, particularly to me—whose husband was murdered for his beliefs, who had legal weapons and political power with which to assert them, and even then had to fly the country and whose beloved daughter has left the country with her husband to spread new learning in a new world—yet there is a sense in which I live beneath these storm clouds, which pass constantly over me, whose rains fall round me and by which I remain untouched. My life and my world spring from within me.

European wars, royal intrigues, exploration beyond the seas, Parliament at war with the throne, Catholic versus Protestant, these hardly touch me, and I view them from afar—brilliant canvasses by skilled artists, awesome, but not real; or else children at play on a nursery floor, each seeing and asserting their rights, and feeling their power over each other.

Wednesday 13th February

The New World

(Bridget)* I think I must write of this not in terms of the little ships of life that sail away across our oceans and find new worlds, returning sometimes with treasures of gold and perfumes and spices (and tea) and new vegetables, and foods with forks, and potatoes! But the whole outreach into new worlds of science and medicine and astronomy and mathematics—all worlds beyond my understanding, and only fragments of this knowledge filter through to me down here in the Forest. Every visit to London takes me into a new world for since the Plague and the Great Fire it has grown and is growing so rapidly that I feel a Stranger there. I feel our old world and our old way of life is having to give way to something new

27

and strange, unknown and frightening. Are we destroying ourselves in all this change? The old rhythm of the seasons, our pastoral life, the framework of our days, our inter-dependent village and town communities are being invaded by new worlds and ways from without. New learning and exploration breed both courage and fear, and I am afraid, for it seems we blind ourselves to God, and have such pride in ourselves and our achievements and judgement. I fear the judgement of man.—

Thursday 14th February

—I think I fear, too, my own ignorance, for, although I read, and teach my household to do the same, and although books and pamphlets and newsheets come my way, even down here, through friends and Robert Whitaker and my London contacts through my husband's old friends, yet I am neither student nor scholar, and am easily confused, bewildered and perplexed. For me, a new world is revealed through my study of the Bible and the insights even the simplest folk in our community throw on the scriptures there. New thought, new life, new worlds come this way for me, always growing and changing. Especially since Sir John's death, for in those days I tried so loyally to support him and be a good wife, following his lead and obeying and often agreeing without thought, and secretly afraid of his hates and distrusts and strong, fierce nature. What freedom to find my own way I now have!

But—New Worlds—and Bridget* following her husband to build and spread new learning through a university away across the ocean, over the edge of our world! The edges of my world are misty, hazy and unreal.

St. Valentine's Day to-day! Merriment among the youngsters and heart-shaped lavender cakes!

Friday 15th February

My thoughts must now be assembled, on Religion and Prayer and the Priesthood.

Here I hardly dare write, even in the privacy of this diary.

Religion

I have a religion. I believe in God. I neither know Him nor

understand Him nor could describe nor explain Him, but I feel Him, through and through me and through and through His world and His people. Known and unknown, seen and unseen, I feel Him with senses deeper and surer than touch or sight. I believe our religious wars, divisions, sects, wranglings, persecutions and struggles are because, far beyond words, each of us feel Him in our own souls. How can I tell you how He feels to me? I can only speak of Him to you, in words, if you know how He feels to you. You cannot force me, or anyone else, to feel Him. Your sword will not open my eyes to see Him, nor will your prison bars or executioner's axe separate me from Him. So, the Bible can lead me to Him, for there are the stories of others who have felt Him, and in Jesus the miracles of feeling, of touch, of every sense. (But this is not physical seeing, touching, tasting, hearing, scenting, but deep feeling of the spirit, and physical senses are only a shadow of the truth of God.)—

Saturday 16th February

—Yes—that's what I feel! That's what we share in our Sunday conventicle. That's why so much of our prayer together is, like the Quakers, in silence—a deep silence which we feel together and where we feel the presence of God. That's why I can only pick phrases out of the Book of Common Prayer, for I will not pray be rote, and there is much there beyond my feeling. Yet, (I hardly dare write this!)—there is much beauty and sincerity there and I know that many of those great scholars who presented it to the King could accept and agree with what I wrote yesterday. But I cannot accept it as the only, true, prayer of the Church of God. Prayer is a deep inward sense of God.

So—to

The Priesthood!

—What a medley of men! Saints and scolars and stupids and sinners! I have met them all! Bishops, priests and deacons! Young, old, pompous and proud, humble and human! The same as the rest of us! I cannot feel they are more speciall 'called' by God than Harriet is 'called' to serve me (for she feels her calling deeply). We are all 'called'. We do not all obey or follow our calling, but I would more readily

29

kneel and kiss Harriet's hand for obedience to her calling than kiss all priestly hands, whether friends or strangers.—

Sunday 17th February

—I want to write more about the priesthood, because they seem to stand apart from society in a strange way, and I have known so many of them well and they have so often poured out their hearts to me, and they are all so different, and the problems of their calling so varied. It is a hard and demanding and cruel way of life, full of bluff and pretence and power and pomp and always the world looks up to (or down on) them and they can never be overlooked, but must be leaders whether they feel like it or not.

I watched a snail in the garden to-day. He was early awake in first sunshine, climbing a wall and then on to the ivy. "You're like a priest!" I thought. "You carry on your back that great load. It is part of you and you cannot live without it. But it makes movement so difficult for you and your fragile, weak self within could not survive without this hard, camouflaged shell. And when you are frightened, or winter winds are cold, you go within and hide yourself away." And as I watched and thought, my snail hauled himself over the ivy leaf, and then pushed out his horns with their penetrating eyes at the tip, and he looked so all-seeing, all-knowing, all-powerful, and I was angry at his pomposity and touched him with a blade of grass and he sped indoors, all timid and afraid, and only the hard, beautiful shell of his kind was left for me to see. He was still a snail!—This priest! But there was something about the lack of any feeling in that shell that spoke to me, too, about the priests' desire to keep part of themselves always hidden from the rest of humankind. From fear and weakness, not from spirituality and strength. The man is imprisoned by the priest, and so is separate from the rest of us. There is desire and longing and hunger within that shell and an inner life, of 'prayer and communion and contemplation'. But, outwardly, they offer us words, reasons, dogmas, theologies, of all shades. These are necessary, but— of what use to the folk of Ibsley, Linwood, Harbridge, Ellingham, Rockford?

So—Prayer—What dare I write?

Will start on that next.

Monday 18th February

Rather disastrous dinner party this afternoon. Food scarce and indifferent and company very formal and boring. (The Coopers from Breamore and some friends of theirs whom I didn't know.) They left early to get back by dark and I was glad.

They tried to find out whether I thought as Sir John! I would not be drawn into politics!.

Tuesday 19th February

Prayer

"Oh, taste and see how gracious the Lord is." Unbelievable that Mr. South should speak to us on those words last Sunday!—Taste and see—the senses—the deep spiritual sense of being aware, without any doubt, that God is within us, and this is what Jesus meant when He said, "I and the Father are one". Mr. South went far along my road but not as far as I go myself, but this is what prayer is. Tasting, seeing—without doubt, for doubts are dispersed by the reality in the experience as certainly as any simple human sense experience, and only able to be shared with others who have had the experience for themselves. That's why Ellingham congregation fills me with a restlessness, for so many (so many of my Moyles Court household) have had no experience of spirit, and are full of fears and suspicions, of witchcraft and alchemy, of poison potions and superstitions. They clutch each other often in fear for they need that experience of touch to strengthen them. The bread and wine, the taste, in the communion service is either a spiritual sense experience, or an incantation to ward off the evil one.

I've rambled on—for I cannot write of my prayers. Words are no good.

Wednesday 20th February

Family and Households

How we cling together! How we need and depend on each other! How interwoven we are! When one of us leaves or another joins us, the whole pattern alters. When Sir John left for Switzerland how released and freed we were in that

31

London household! As the children grew up and left home how changed those of us who remained were. And the servants, too; every newcomer brings something fresh, even the youngest boy on the farm or in the coach-house or serving-girl in the kitchem. This is not just because I have become over-sensitive to those days of the Civil War and Commonwealth when no one knew whether it was friend or foe, soldier or spy, who craved a night's shelter. I welcomed them all, wherever we were living and never probed to find out where they came from or what their business and they were grateful just to be accepted. Now, here in the Forest, our 'family' is not just those on the Moyles estate but many feel safe here, from as far as Gorley and over the bridge at Harbridge and Bicton, over even to Godshill and Horton they speak of "we". Then there's my meeting group; we need and support each other and care and accept.

Thursday 21st February

Nothing to write! Words spent! A discipline over. Session with my present chaplain to-day and he always makes me feel very small and ignorant and he always counsels caution and reason and the acceptance of the centuries old authority of the Church. I feel deep down he, also, is confused, and clings to logic and reason, with a deep hunger within. Will John Hicks return soon? He said he did not expect to be more than a month away and it is four weeks tomorrow since he was here.

Friday 22nd February

I'm tired of writing my journal in this way, and write more happily and freely when I just recall my days and doings and the thoughts that interest me that I cannot share with others. I learnt to cope with my loneliness in this way a long time ago—in the days of the Civil War and Commonwealth when I struggled to be loyal to my, sometimes frightening, husband, and when I lived in fear—for his life, for his friends, for my friends, and our home and when London was all gossip, slander, argument, brawl and quarrel. And the children were young, but old enough to be caught in the adult world of intrigue and war, and I was anxious and wondered if they could ever grow up with sound views and morals and beliefs of

32

their own. I remember in family prayers, one day, when Sir John was away, a friend of our coachman prayed fervently, "O God, save the King," and Sir John came home and next morning prayed, "Oh God, remove from among us this false king who would defy his people," and I was so afraid young John would tell his father of our prayers the day before and I would be accused of being a Royalist! Those days are mercifully past and we have new freedom. At least I can write my thoughts—though am not in favour of anyone reading them!

Saturday 23rd February

He came to-day! But, so briefly. He arrived at noon and left again just before dark as he reached Portsmouth a week ago, and is going through to Devon, mostly to see his flock at Kingsbridge, but calling in at Lyme where he has many friends. Oh, John, my dear, dear, John! He was at his most strong and beautiful, looking less tired and strained and he said his visit to France had been "very valuable", "fruitful", "encouraging". I ask few questions for I want him to feel free, and I have to hold back my anxiety and curiosity about why he must always be restless and on the move. What is happening in France? He went on to his friends at Ashley Heath and Holt for the night, and did not want to be seen in Ringwood. I gave him a rabbit pie and roast pigeons and thick vegetable soup before he left, and he asked me not to tell the meeting to-morrow that he had been here. (But I'm afraid they will hear through those in the household who saw him.)

Was able to tell him of my 'death' in the bog three weeks ago and he understood.

Sunday 24th February

I had so hoped John Hicks would be here for our meeting to-day, and it was very difficult to say nothing of his visit. There was talking amongst a group of them after, and they went silent as I came near; it was the Linwood group and I felt they had heard he had been. They find me rather formidable so dared say nothing direct and, for once, I was glad to be rather remote and so keep my secret. (?) Even in our group, where we have been able to share our hopes and beliefs and doubts so much more than in usual congregations, distrusts and suspicions arise.

Monday 25th February

I rode over to Linwood in the morning with a basket of pasties and bread for the poor Ashly family. But it was partly an excuse to visit Janet and her husband as I knew they would mention John Hicks' visit if they had heard. All was well and my mind was set at rest for they were welcoming and there was no suspicion. Had thought of going on to Fritham Lodge, but it began to rain hard and the forest tracks were so slippery and muddy and the days are still too short for me happily to have gone home by the gravel track over by Hampton Ridge. So, back soon after noon and a quiet evening indoors as drizzle set in. Took the nice young Bob with me to Linwood; he is so proud of his father who is a sailor, so rarely at home. He brought his falcon with him and had it flying well, (so we brought a rabbit back!) Bob talked incessantly—"Father says...." "Father told me...." "When father gets back—!" He is only staying with us until summer. I suppose there is a chance, with the Dutch wars over, that his father might come home soon.

Tuesday 26th February

Unbelievable! Who should turn up to-day—unannounced, and unexpected? Young Bulstrode Whitelocke! After all these years! He has been staying with the Shaftesburys and was on his way back to Chilton Park. A horseman galloped in at near mid-day to announce his coming and for a moment I expected father not son—and they duly arrived!—Three carriages, and a wagon came up later with luggage and furniture and servants for he had been staying there with his beagle pack for over three weeks. I recognised him for he is like his father who is now, he says, very frail and ill. It was good to see him, and hear of Sir Bulstrode who was my first love so many years ago.

It is over 25 years since we met, when he was so wretched because of the insanity of his wife, and I so troubled and lonely as Sir John was so often away and so wedded to his politics and the Commonwealth, and I could never be happy in

London. Bulstrode was my great support and love. He was never strong, and I remember, in anguish for him when he was ill, consulting William Lilly, the great astrologer, as to whether he would recover.

I persuaded young Bulstrode to stay for a night and he agreed. Great consternation as there were ten servants with him, and the beagles! The family is in financial straits, but—not surprising, with all those 18 children.

Wednesday 27th February

A noisy night of singing and music in the servants' quarters, while Bulstrode and I sat over the fire and he told me of his father and their poverty and his new third wife.

He sang airs from the masques at Court and some of his father's tunes and songs and I pretended I was shocked and he said "My father always called you the Puritan Maid!" And I said, "I'm wiser now, and the country is always more understanding of honest fun than the towns, which make all things lewd and bawdy!"

Sir Bulstrode is permanently now at Chilton Park,* no longer Keeper of the Great Seal or holding any public office, and is obviously very unwell, tires easily and eats little.

They packed up and went off in the late morning, hoping to be home by dark. Young Bulstrode begged me to visit his father. He has done a lot of building at Chilton and would be interested in my plans to build on here. I think I must visit him. I have many strange memories of the affair of our youth, and I was very emotionally stirred by his son's coming. Sir Bulstrode steered a shrewd path between monarchism and republicanism—much more political than religious.

Thursday 28th February

More thoughts of Bulstrode. Occasionally Sir John mentioned him—sneeringly—and they were acquaintances as Keepers of the Great Seal but far from friends. Bulstrode's youthful faith in freedom of conscience has always been part of his basic philosophy and this would never have suited my autocratic husband's determination to manipulate the King, the parliament and me. Young Bulstrode spoke movingly on Tuesday night of his father's beloved second wife, his mother,

Frances, (and their dozen and a half children) and he had years of happiness with her. I remembered sadly the distance that always lay between Sir John and me, though I could share Sir Bulstrode's joy in his children, for it is in motherhood that my fulfilment has always been. Hearing Bulstrode speak of his father's life and his children (one in Turkey) made me realise again the tempestuous age in which we have lived—unrest, strife and new horizons opening to New Worlds, across oceans, and through science, mathematics, medicine—far more than the human soul can grasp, and so full of danger. I walked towards Fritham alone in the early afternoon to quieten my feelings and mind and found peace again in the watery sunset, and returned to my "family" and was grateful for their loyal acceptance of me. (Bulstrode told me very entertainingly about his father's time in Stockholm as Ambassador and his contact with Queen Christina—he kept a diary as I do).

MARCH

Friday 1st March

What a hectic week! All straight again after the Whitelock visit!—New Rushes laid, carpet swept, floors polished and peace reigns again! It was good to hear old Bellman playing his fiddle in the kitchen and the others singing!—Better than the noise of young Bulstrode's party, many of whom were drunken louts, and I was quite relieved when they left, and we could settle down again. We are very overcrowded when visitors come.

Bellman has picked up some of the airs young Bulstrode had sung—of his father's, from the old days of his masques at court. Strange that I should hear his tunes around me again after twenty five years!

Saturday 2nd March

Heavy rain all day and the ford impassable, but the woods full of snowdrops and bluebells bursting through by the path down Ellingham Drove. Ibsley meadows flooded and no way through to Harbridge until they go down. Flocks of swans and geese on the water and plovers calling and curlew and sandpiper. Walked that way and was turned back by flood water, but spent time watching the water at Ibsley bridge, and puzzling about the times in which we live—all argument and wrangling and discord and little peace, little understanding and little love.

No day passes without John H. close to my heart and mind.

Sunday 3rd March

Rev. Compton South came over last night and took our meeting today. He came yesterday just before dark—thank goodness he didn't come last week!—to share a newsletter, handwritten, that he had received from London about a Mr. John Bunyan. He has been in prison because of his beliefs, but was released over a year ago. He is trying to help the simple, newly literate folk to understand that Bible stories may have a metaphorical meaning and we must look behind facts for deeper truth. Fiction is untruth, but metaphor is truth, and we must search for truth. He is writing of a journeying Christian struggling not to conform to this world and lose his integrity by trying to please others or impress by argument.

Mechanical answers are useless to a feeling, suffering, person, and we must shake off priestly domination and find our own freedom, and have faith in our own insights. This Mr. Bunyan was a tinker—fought in the Civil War, and is one of, what I call, the "new" Christians who seem to me, in the purposes of God, to rise up to help us in our Gospel search and to help our barriers of wealth and poverty to fall away as we search for our own theology.

Monday 4th March

Marvellous early spring day! The winter is, dare I believe it, nearly over. The kitchen staff are all coughing and sneezing and I'm going round them morning and evening with coltsfoot mixture and an ointment with camphor. I made mint and treacle candy today to try to cheer them and we all gathered after lunch and drank hot punch over the kitchen hob and we laughed and our spirits were lifted. Then the house smelt so strongly of mint and ale and camphor that I went out to walk in the fields—on the gravel path they made last autumn which has miraculously survived the floods and walking was reasonably dry. Thoughts of the new building. I must seriously get down to it now the days are lengthening.

Tuesday 5th March

Warm winds and sunshine and I decided to ride over to Harbridge and, if the floods were down enough, to go on to Fordingbridge, by the high track to Bicton Mill. Found Margaret at home with James and Jenny, and Robert gone to Salisbury. She was in the garden and we did some cutting back and tying and staking together. She is very loyal to Robert, who seems to me either very confused or not very articulate! He says some odd things and then contradicts them as if the echoes of his first remark reach him much later and he hears their inadequacy and struggles to put it right without losing face. Margaret always stands by him but is well aware that I am a critical mother-in-law!

Thursday 7th March

Nothing happened yesterday or to-day, but the sun shone! How can I say nothing happened if the sun shone!—That miraculous happening, especially when its warmth marks the end of winter! Walked by the Dockens through the woods. How the winds have pruned the trees! I came back with a great armful of kindling and branches and was met by the stable boys who rushed up to take my load and carry it back for me. They were specially eager and friendly because of the candy making on Tuesday! Baby Tom was crawling in the puddles and I picked him up bawling, and carried him in to that feckless little serving girl who is his mother, and Harriet chided me with, "Oh madam!" when she saw the state of my dress covered with mud and torn by brambles.

Friday 8th March

Spent the day staking and tying in the garden—the rambling roses and lupins now growing fast and the tulips. Clipped back rosemary and lavender and planted out white violets that I've had indoors all winter. John Evelyn's almanac for gardeners, which is at Wilton House, is full of helpful ideas. He left them a copy nearly twenty years ago when he was touring England and stayed for the Hare Coursing on Salisbury plain. They have used it in their gardens and glass-houses for many years and I copied many parts that have been very useful to me—like keeping white violets indoors, and they have flowered all the winter. Flood water subsiding but a bitter wind rocking the elms and oaks and strewing the drive with branches. The musk roses from last year look strong and are shooting well. Pruned them back.

Saturday 9th March

Lovely discovery today. Harriet took down the damask hangings in the Beconshaw bed-chamber to shake them in the garden and re-hang them for the summer, and I took advantage of the window lights to turn out the old chest which was full of things from London and the Isle of Wight* and brought here before the Civil War for safe keeping, and before I came back to live here. There were some of the children's outgrown clothes which I laid aside to give away in the village, but I found an old copy of Milton's poems and translations given me by my husband. I sat on the edge of the chest and got lost in the beauty of his words which might have been written for us here. Will copy here Psalm 1 done into verse 1653—

> "Blest is the man who has not walked astray
> In counsel of the wicked, and in the way
> Of sinners hath not stood, and in the seat
> Of scorners hath not sat; but in the great
> Jehovah's Law he studies day and night.
> He shall be as a tree which planted grows
> By watery streams, and in his season knows
> To yield his fruit; and his leaf shall not fall,
> And what he takes in hand shall prosper all".

And Psalm 84—beautiful—and so much more that I had forgotten (or never read!)

Harriet caught me reading in the dusk and dust!—Helped me clear up and repack the chest.

Sunday 10th March

But—took the Milton up to my room. How could he, who was such a heavy scholar, such a disciplined stern Puritan, statesman, politician, reach down to the simple understanding of folk like me?—And now he is and has been for many years, blind—and yet so far-sighted.

40

Ps.84.

How lovely are thy dwellings fair!	—Our chapel meeting place
O Lord of Hosts, how dear	
The pleasant tabernacles are	
Where thou dost dwell so near	
My soul doth long and almost die	—The buildings & sanctuaries are dead, for the life of God is spirit.
Thy courts, O Lord, to see;	
My heart and flesh aloud to cry	
O living God for thee	
There even the sparrow, freed from wrong	
Hath found a house of rest;	
The swallow there to lay her young	—We had them in our chapel eaves last summer.
Hath built her brooding nest,	
Even by thy altars, Lord of Hosts,	
They find their safe abode;	
And home they fly from round the coasts	—Folk come all around to our conventicle.
T'ward thee, my King, my God.	

Monday 11th March

Sent the old waggon with Bob and Bellman and William to Fordingbridge to buy fish and potatoes. We grew a few and they have been a success and they have grown a good crop of them at Breamore for the first time and will let me have some, if I collect them before the Penruddocks from Hale arrive! Sent a note to Margaret suggesting they keep the waggoners overnight and she and the children come back with them for the day to-morrow. We could see them back on horseback as far as Harbridge and they could walk home from there before dark.

Tuesday 12th March

So, Margaret came over for the day from Fordingbridge with the children. We crossed the Dockens and went up through the woods to the Cuckoo Pines, the children running wildly ahead and climbing into the trees to look for the sea. James is a lovely child, but very headstrong and disobedient. Children need so much freedom, but our society is determined that they shall be little, obedient, conforming adults. I read Ben Jonson on Education to Margaret and discussed the importance of what he says, for she scolds and punishes her children for small things. I think fear of her husband makes her do this—fear that he will disapprove of her laxity.

Jonson says: "Do not tell him all his faults, lest you make him grieve and faint and at last despair. For nothing doth more hurt than to make him so afraid of all things as he can endeavour nothing . . . If you pour a glut of water upon a bottle, it receives little of it; but with a funnel by degrees, you shall fill many and spill little of your own; to their capacity they will all receive and be full." Margaret says "Yes, yes, how wise!" And almost at once shouted at James, "Bow James, when you leave your grandmother's presence. When will you learn the manners of a gentleman!"

Wednesday 13th March

Yesterday was good and I was glad Robert could not come. I do not often get Margaret on her own. We rode to Harbridge after the meal, James behind me on Molly, and Margaret with little Jenny on Captain and Ken followed on foot to ride Captain back and escort me. We stopped at Ibsley Bridge and the water meadows were still flooded. James counted twenty-six Bewick Swans and there were six Canada geese* by the weir and peewits were calling. We shall get plovers' eggs any time now, reminding me always of spring in the Isle of Wight, so long ago. In the end we rode as far as Bicton Mill which would mean they only had about 2 miles to walk, and it was a superb evening and I loved the leisurely ride home in the sunset, with Ken whistling Bulstrode's tunes! How my staff took to those melodies and how they enjoyed that whole hectic visit!

Thursday 14th March

A messenger came today with a note that delighted and excited me from Bulstrode Whitelocke from Chilton Foliat. Apparently young Bulstrode left many of his things at Gussage St. Giles with the Ashley Coopers, expecting to return. He has now gone to London to join in the Dryden masques at

Court, so they are sending a coach down to collect his property. Bulstrode invites me to return with the coach and he will see me home again after a few days visit. I (at sixty!) am delighted, and will go! Bulstrode said, "You will find me much changed—I am a sick man, with little strength left. It was given to my country which never trusted me, and I am now at Chilton Lodge where you would be a welcome visitor. The house is in some confusion of repair and disrepair for I have had to fight against destruction in the timbers from beetle, discovered when I had nearly completed my building. Now I am forced to do repairs I cannot afford. But come, dear friend, and we will recall our youth and happiness together" . . . and more!

So I arranged that the coach will return here for the night of March 17th and return to Chilton with me on the 18th.

I'm sixty! And feel a young girl at heart again!

Friday 15th March

Sent Ken to Ringwood first thing to catch the post with a letter to Bulstrode, as I know the Oxford post goes by Newbury, to tell him that I will accept his invitation. Will we manage it in one day? I have suggested he returns me to Salisbury only, and I will spend the night of Saturday at Wilton House. So a letter to Anne* to tell her my plans and my hopes of staying with her until Monday. I laughed at myself as I found myself busy working out this and that scheme, which was the effect Bulstrode always had on me. So unlike Sir John, for with him I always did as I was told, quickly, efficiently, but no plan was ever my own! It was the same when I wrote to William Lilly,* about Bulstrode in 1643. My idea, and he the incentive! I do look forward to seeing him and cannot imagine him old and sick and penniless!

I hope Anne will be at Wilton for I am fond of her and she knows Bulstrode well.

Saturday 16th March

Much to do to leave Moyles Court smooth running while I am away. My staff is good just now and I feel, with Harriet and Pilbeam all will be well. The new gamekeeper seems a real asset and keeps strict guard over the guns and stands no non-

43

sense from the young men. I shall probably take Ken with me. He is so good with horses and will be a help if anything goes wrong. His second wife is sweet and just as willing as Ken, but they are having trouble with Phyllis, now sixteen, and very flighty, as her mother, his first wife was. She chases all the young men and is very restless and careless.

Sunday 17th March

Told Rev. John Crofts that I would be away next weekend. It was hard to concentrate at meeting in the morning. My mind was full of packing and what I should take! (Most unsuitable thoughts on a Sunday for a leader of a conventicle!) John Crofts preached on "Put not your trust in riches or in any child of man", and I was glad I only need confess my sins to God and not to any priest for God knows how easily Rev. Crofts would have filled me with fear and guilt, and I do not see my wandering thoughts as sin. So my thoughts wandered! Should I take my green flannel gown with yellow sleeved bodice or the black satin with lace? Or both?

I can only take one chest for there is no waggon mentioned, so I cannot take much. Must remember wooden pattens, unless Bulstrode is not strong enough to show me round his estate. I wonder what his third wife is like, and how much changed he will be or find me, now we are both old! Only the existence of young Bulstrode made me feel old!—An exaggeration, almost a caricature, of his delightful, attractive father at that age.

Monday 18th March

To Chilton Foliat

The coach from St. Giles arrived before dark last night and was ready to leave soon after breakfast. Harriet had been bustling around finding this and tidying that, pulling my laces and fussing, and I was ready when the coach came round. I could see no sign in it of the things that young Bulstrode had left and when I asked the coachman he said, "It is things of a lady's heart, we collected, my Lady!—Jewels and trinkets and pearls and a ring with diamonds. It seems our young master had changed his mind when he reached home and sent us back to collect his misplaced gifts! The lady flung them at us when she read his note and her eyes were full of tears. But—they are young, and we all make mistakes when we're young." (And I remembered our mistakes when we were young!. And I setting off now to be reminded of them!)

"The treasures are under the coachman's seat, my Lady, for safety!" And they packed in my luggage, and Ken rode outside, and Phyllis came too, to wait on me. Joanna can't manage her when Ken is away.

They had two men riding alongside, and so we set off for Salisbury.

And I left this diary behind—locked away in the Bible box. If Bulstrode had seen it he would have asked to read it. (He used to keep one, I remember!) I couldn't have refused him— so I "forgot" it on purpose.

Tuesday 19th March

(These days are written as I look back over this delightful, happy week. A blue-washed, warm week of spring sunshine, gilded grasses and young life.) We changed horses at some coaching inn at lunch-time and had mulled ale, bread and cheese. Picked up Bulstrode's team, who knew they were going home and went well, quickly through the edge of Savernake Forest, known to harbour highwaymen. Then, Chilton Foliat—and we met! He is grey, and stooped and tottering, with a stick and a man-servant to support him. Our eyes met (his still twinkling) and how we laughed! And years fell away as we laughed! It was dark as we arrived and the lights were in when I came down, changed and freshened. His wife (third) was pleasant and gracious—much younger than us—more in common with young Bulstrode, I suspect, than her husband. (I suspect an affair there?) There were four other "children"—young men and maids—at home, and we had food and wine in his lovely dining room. Beautiful house, but obvious signs of major repairs having recently been done and much left undone. "I have had to rebuild the back entirely," he said, "It was uninhabitable." . . . "Now the rest must be done after my day when these sons have made some money of their own and stopped squandering mine."

45

Wednesday 20th March

I spent the morning with Mary, who was very unsure of me. B. had made much of his friendship with Sir John, and I, merely "his poor widow!" We went in the kitchens and dairy and visited the stables and barns, the smithy and bakehouse, and I felt Mary was insecure, in spite of 8 children. It must be hard for her to take the place of Frances; Bulstrode was so happy in that marriage, and there was money then and prosperity and success. Bulstrode stays in bed until midday. It felt at this point as if I should have no chance to see him alone, and the purpose of my visit was to give him comfort and remind him of his vigorous, important, varied, past—as politician, writer, traveller, and much respected person. I did just that, when he joined us in the afternoon. He took me (always with his supporting man-servant) to see the restored part of the house, which has been beautifully done, with massive beams and brickwork covered with canvas and plaster, and decorated plaster ceilings.

Music in the evening and Bulstrode sang and Mary played the spinet. "Call in the staff if they want to come!" he said and I heard a bell clang in the yard (from the bell foundry in the village) which brought about ten or twelve of his household and he has obviously trained them to sing madrigals, folksongs and some rousing (men only) songs of the taverns. He got rather drunk and over-excited and had to be carried off to bed! Oh, Bulstrode, you don't change! For all that shrewd politician that you let the world think you really were!

Thursday 21st March

A very happy day!—Still spring in the air, sunshine and warmth. Mary went to market in the morning; she didn't suggest I went too. She saw me as an old lady, no longer able to keep up for a long day!—Just when I was feeling so rejuvenated! But, we were lunching at Littlecote House, so I was quite glad to stay behind. Bulstrode must have heard I was alone for he came down just before noon, and we had wine together looking over Chilton Park for nearly an hour before Mary returned and we had to get ready for luncheon. Happy, relaxed, easy talking together and B. outpoured so much— grief at Frances' death, despair over young Bulstrode, disappointment over Mary, anxiety over penury and ill-health, disgust at the end of the Commonwealth, the Restoration, the unnecessary and ever widening gulf caused by Catholic and Protestant rivalry, the King's laws for both tightening and relaxing his hold—always precarious. "I would try the New World if I were younger!" he said. No chance to tell him of my problems!—My role was to hear of his, and I was glad he had this need of me. He still writes a lot.

The luncheon at Littlecote was impressive and formal and very grand. I played "Dame Alice Lisle" with careful attention to detail and didn't let B-W down!

Friday 22nd March

The last day! There was a great invasion of the Crokes from Newbury in the afternoon. Young (not now very young!) Unter and his wife. Uncle George died some years ago, but Uncle John is alive. Unter has kept in touch with Bulstrode as he went with him to Sweden. He knew my husband, and is cousin to Catherine, of the Dibden crowd. I get confused over all these relations. And was hopelessly lost over Bulstrode's eighteen children!!—Without the Crokes as well! We went out again to see the horses, and B has an old, old horse Cromwell gave him. He's very old now and B can't bear to have him put down, wise old horse!—How does he see the world he has lived in? Has he a memory?

The Crokes left at about 4pm and Bulstrode was tired and went up for an hour's rest. The younger children came in from shooting in the park, "famished" they said, and good smells came from the kitchen. We had a happy meal, three of the boys and a daughter ate with us. (Young Bulstrode had found a note after his return to say the girl he courted never wanted to see him again. Hence the coach trip and young B. to London and the court!)

The Duke of Monmouth is back from France—in the King's favour again. John H. has met him. I think his visits to France were somehow connected with the Duke.

Saturday 23rd March

Bulstrode insisted on coming with me to Wilton. He was keen to see the rebuilding of the house since the fire. He assured

Mary it would be restful and a change for him. So away we went—with four outriders and it was a very moving and delightful journey through the Wiltshire villages. Phyllis was in the coach with us, but indifferent to our conversation having so much of her own affairs to think about. We spoke of my Moyles Court conventicle; he was relieved that I had the King's authority for this, and seemed rather unhappy about my being so open and unafraid.

I told him I was planning to build a new wing on the house, but I let the conversation drop, as Bulstrode is sensitive about his penury and inability to go on building at Chilton. He spoke of the need for a good architect and, like a man, made it sound beyond the power of a woman to achieve!

We reached Wilton just before dark, going slowly, with tired horses at the end. Anne gave us a great welcome, and I was so glad she was at home and had had my note. Had splendid meal, and sat over the wine and fruit, till B. (whose man-servant was clearly anxious about him), said he must retire. Anne and I stayed up late, talking, talking. The Earl is a sick man, and Anne worried about him, so I never saw him, and I missed the remarkable old Countess now back in the north.

Sunday 24th March

Bulstrode left, soon after he came down, near noon. He gave me a long hold as he kissed my hand. "You seem to know each other well!" Anne said as the coach disappeared. "Yes," I said, "but we have met very little!" I realised he had hardly had time to notice the house though he said that that was why he came! We wandered round those marvellous grounds and the huge house, so beautifully restored and cared for, and Anne asked me to go with her to Salisbury Cathedral for the service there. I was a little anxious, but I was her visitor, so we went—in her lovely little fashionable carriage. What did that experience do to me? The Cathedral is so vast, that little men are dwarfed, and priests and vestments, and pomp and ritual are all shrunken, and the majesty and glory of those great arches and high windows and carved roof cannot fail to speak of God. As long as I looked up, I could worship God, and the music went up with me—and it was real. (As long as I kept my head high and my gaze away from the human level.) So I was able to thank Anne for taking me there, and felt that the Cathedral could, perhaps, hold Christendom together. I was glad I had my black satin, though Anne looked splendidly fashionable in dark blue taffeta with a grey plume in her hat—which she said was less colourful than her usual dress, but "it was Lent, and the purples of the Church would go well". Oh, dear!

Monday 25th March

My carriage back to Moyles came before noon. All was well at Moyles Court, except for a bad fire, not far from Betty Smithers—old Kate's cottage gutted, and Betty took the poor old thing in, badly shaken, but unhurt. So I set off from Wilton after luncheon, with Ken obviously glad to be going home, and Phyllis as always full of herself. And so—home. I, too, glad to be back, but with very happy memories—and much to fill in in this diary.

Tuesday 26th March

A day picking up the threads and writing of the last week in here. So much I want to write! I shall never forget our journey from Chilton Foliat to Wilton. Bulstrode seemed to know the road so well and pointed out all the new manor houses recently built, and the ancient churches, and we went through strings of little villages with reed-thatched cottages and mills—for we followed the Kennet and Avon rivers most of the way.

It was all new to me after we left the Moat House at Downton. Going north we followed the Post road, for safety. Salisbury plain is deserted with large farmlands, and the road kept to the rivers and villages whenever possible. My travels have taken me to Winchester and London but, except for Salisbury, this was new territory to me.

Wednesday 27th March

Nothing to write! Still busy on these last pages!—A damp drizzly day—after this marvellous last week of sunshine. Bulstrode said the Hungerfords* owned land at Great Durnford, but never lived there.

Thursday 28th March

They have worked so hard while I have been away. The kitchen garden has been prepared and all the cabbage and spinach seeds are planted and onion sets in. Pilbeam has tidied the timber stacks knowing we shall need them in order if we start to build, and the girls have been spring cleaning. I'm very pleased with them all—even James Dunne who brought me a clay pipe he had made! I think he had hoped I might bring him tobacco from Chilton Park, since apparently young Bulstrode showed off his ability to smoke it when he was here. A dangerous habit though said to be good for the health.

The beans are coming up and climbing sticks placed for them, but pigeons causing trouble.

Friday 29th March

Last night Robert Whitaker came over with Margaret bringing with him a poem of George Herbert's just published in Salisbury. We sat till dusk reading it together, and he has left it with me till he is coming by again. It brought back to me that wonderful meeting with him years ago. (Was I seventeen or eighteen?) I visited Bemerton with my father who left me with Mr. and Mrs. Herbert while he visited the weavers at Wilton. As we drove up the drive I heard him playing the lute and singing—gentle and rhythmic and lovely, with interruptions and repetitions and I guessed he was building up a song of his own. Mrs. Herbert took me into his study. He was a lovely person, warm, young, handsome, with quick movements, quick laughter and "meeting" eyes. He showed me his unfinished poem, "Teach me my God and King, In all things thee to see . . ." and I felt he saw God and good in me. The verse that begins "A man that looks on glass," etc. was alive in front of me and I felt he saw deep into my heart, as my God does. There was a lovely penetration about him that made a "meeting" between us that was rare and special. He has been very close to me ever since, though he died that year after.

Saturday 30th March

George Herbert vividly recalled to me by this new poem. My meeting with him, so briefly, all those forty years ago had much to do with forming my spiritual understanding of the Christ in each of us, of the Holy Spirit moving deep between us. He spoke of the Catholic Church as a bride over-dressed and the Calvinist Church as the stripped and naked bride— and, I remember, he picked up his lute and sang again, about the stained glass in Bemerton Church. (Glass, and seeing through things, was a very close and meaningful symbol that day—to him and me.)

Over forty years ago and a deep impressiosn and memory of it with me still and still creative.

The new poem Robert W. brought is full and speaks as surely to me now as Mr. Herbert did then. Called "The Sacrifice", and full of the agony of our struggling, divided, antagonisms in the religious wars of these days. He sees it as the repetition of the pain Jesus knew at his arrest, through his trials and to his crucifixion. "Was ever grief like mine?"

"Oh all ye who pass by, whose eyes and minde
To worldly things are sharp, but to me blinde;
To me, who took eyes that I might you finde:
        Was ever grief like mine?

And on and on. Each stanza live and real. Wept copiously for our own blindness to each other. "They lay hold on me not with the hands of faith, but fury."

Sunday 31st March

Meeting this morning in my chapel. Fourteen of us and we read of Jesus feeding the multitudes. He feeds us all and we snatch and grasp at our food, greedy, as if only we were fed and all others he sent empty away. Catholic food, Calvinist food, Puritan food. Protestant, Presbyterian, Anglican, all kinds of people; we struggle for ourselves, for our own meat and drink. "To worldy things are sharp, but to me blinde." We met this morning, not to meet each other, though we give each other strength and support and comfort, but to reach out to God, and through our Lord's resurrection to see more clearly. I cannot dwell on our sins, as the Calvinists. I cannot waste time on symbols of light or colour or liturgy or music or priestly hierarchy as the churches do. It is the God within me that I would know—the resurrected God in Jesus who, when

51

he was alone, flamed up in light and fire, and this burned in him and lighted those around him. I think John Hicks will be with us next Sunday—from Oxford, where he has been for Easter with his brother George—and he is going on to Dorchester. He and I share so much understanding though I could be his mother. Do hope he comes. Ellingham for even-song, but feel hopelessly out of harmony there and seems to watch each grain slip through the hour glass!

APRIL

Monday 1st April

All Fools' Day! A day in honour of us all, for we are all so foolish, and never more so than when se set ourselves up as judges of each other, knowing nothing and thinking we are right!

Tuesday 2nd April

A dreadful brawl in the kitchens and court-yard last night. Once again, a handful of youths, drunk, fell in the Dockens' Water and turned up dripping wet to dry themselves before going home. Pat and Philip and Thomas and poor young James sat with them at the fireside and Patrick said something about them being "fools lost in the forest", after All Fools Day revelling, and one of the young men drew a knife and started an affray. Philip has a gash on his arm and the women have torn doublets and hose to mend and my pot of soup was spilt in the fire and the smell of burning is all over the back of the house. But—they were driven off over the ford on to the field path at last. My men are good and strong—all eight of them were finally in the fray. But Ken Ostler brought old rope and their hands were tied behind their backs for their journey home. (Home? Or were they vagrants?) They say one of the brawlers had just returned from being apprenticed to a builder in London and those apprentices gang up together and there are brawls and violence, and vandalism and thieving goes on among them. London still struggling through the rubble and aftermath of the Fire, and new building going on everywhere, and young people out of control.

Thursday 4th April

Francis Bacon: "Poetry is a part of Learning, in measure of words, for the most part retained, but, in all other points, extremely licensed, and doth truly refer to the imagination,

53

which, being not tied to the laws of matter, may at pleasure join that which Nature hath severed, and sever that which Nature hath joined, and so we make unlawful matches and divorces of things." These words comfort me for I have immense faith in my vivid and active imagination which gives me insight into people and their behaviour and motivation far more valid and convincing than the experiments and struggles of science and mathematics. It is a marvellous and fearsome time to be alive! Life teems all round and thoughts of men fly down so many new ways.

I drove to Dibden and on with Catherine* to Lymington where ships were being loaded to cross the oceans to strange distant places. The chandlers were hawking spices on the harbour wall and showed us pearls and strange Eastern jewellery. I bought a pennyworth of frankincense—from a sailor who had picked it up on the coast of Arabia. I loved it, for it looked like nothing, but when burnt it will be full of fragrance. Strange treasures about these days—the best being sold for fantastic prices in London and at court.

Friday 5th April

Came back to Fritham Lodge and stayed the night. I got back late this morning to find the blacksmith from Gorley had been to complete the rivetting of the new basket-grate in the hall. The evenings are still cold so we lighted the fire and it blazed warmly and lighted up the date 1674—at the back and it drew well. He must do the iron-work for the new wing as his work is good. Received a message from an architect from Hungerford who will call in tomorrow, sent by Bulstrode. He designed the building and repairs at Chilton Lodge and B. was very satisfied with him. He is working in Salisbury, now, for the Dean and Chapter, so he will know local craftsmen. It was good of Bulstrode to contact him for me and I remember he said he had not used an architect for some years, "being now heavily in debt and unable to use such luxuries." I hope he will not be too expensive, but cheaper architects are in London vying for work in the massive rebuilding going on there.

Saturday 6th April

I think I've got the right architect! His name is Mr. Philip

Webb and he was a pupil of Inigo Jones before Bulstrode had him at Chilton Park. He helped with the building of Wilton House, ages ago, in the '40s, before the Civil War and the awful fire there. He is not young—older than I, I suspect, but I liked him and he seemed quickly to grasp what I wanted. He is advising the Dean and Chapter about restoration and repairs at Salisbury this month but is only advising, so says he will have plenty of time to draw up plans in the next two weeks, and says, if we gather our team of work-people and begin work by mid-May, we should be finished before winter. He can get stone-masons from Salisbury, and knows a carver—ex-pupil of Grinling Gibbons—who will do the interior woodwork, and train our young apprentices. I must find labourers from the estate and contact the brickmakers at Fritham. Thank goodness we have seasoned oak already, even if it's not enough. Son John has plenty stored from the ship-building at Lymington. He ought to spare me some?! Can I trust Pilbeam with all this extra? It is all in addition to the routine and he has started drinking too much. This is all very exciting.

Sunday 7th April

John Hicks came unexpectedly last night. He brought a news-letter from the Dissenters in Oxford. He came very late and slept in the granary again. This is becoming his special place here—among the sacks of grain. He is happy to be undisturbed and can rest. He is a flame to me, burns in me, and I love him dearly. I saw his dim candle flame as I peered through the chink of the shutters on the pannelled landing, and I understood his strengths and his weaknesses and his deep uncertainty about his role as a priest. Can he hold his truth within the priesthood, or must he move, or be thrown out? I feel strangely bound to John Hicks—not just in thinking, but in heart, and in the burning of our spirits, and in our reason for living and dying. I feel I need him, but *why*? Where Where are we bound together except in love of our Lord and in our meetings for prayer? I know in me an inner spring of spirit that grows stronger and stronger—I have known this often before—and it is a power gathering to resist some *shock*. My spirit is strong enough to take it, yet it remains an unexplainable mystery. I watch it like a bubble, but if I touch it, it will break. It appears fragile and is in reality an inner strength, eternal, indestructible. *I* am the fragile bubble that encases it. Shared this with John last night. he listened with quiet respect, but 'I did not feel he understood. Where does he stand?

Monday 8th April

By dawn he had gone. To Portsmouth this time I think. Why? He said he would be back for our next Sunday meeting en route for Dorchester and then to Kingsbridge, this little remote Devon village where has a little group of God-fearing folk. It is "safe", he says, on a river estuary, and he can hide in the creeks and he told me that ships sail to France from Salcombe and he can even row, in a very small boat, to pick up a fishing boat there. But—he never tells me of *what* he is afraid, *what* he is doing, *why* so much going here and there. Is it politics or religion? These two are inseparable and I only know he is motivated by his love of our Lord. This is why he became a priest, but what a stranglehold he feels the priesthood is to him now, for the Church, in Catholic or Anglican form, has rejected him and he cannot accept the dictatorial form of the new Book of Common Prayer. (Oh, I can see its value, and that it was needed, and I can praise those who framed it. And yet, like John, I cannot use it as it should be used.)

Tuesday 9th April

John H's visit—so unexpected—so short—pushed Mr. Webb's visit and plans for building right to the back of my mind. But today I talked it all over with Pilbeam. He is very experienced. Was a soldier in the New Model Army in the Civil War, has trained race-horses for the King at Newbury, had experience of marketing in grain, and is an experienced builder! What more could I want? I feel very blessed to have him here.

I never mentioned the building to John H. He had too much on his mind and his visit was too short. Perhaps next weekend. I shall use Beconshaw money*, for Sir John would not have wanted his money used for anything other than politics. Kings! Parliaments! Commonwealth! Catholics! Protestants!

Great Seals for this and that, and so much treachery and distrust! I see both good and bad in every way I look. Our Ringwood group, our Moyles Court meeting, this is enough. If we can grow together under God, it is all we can do with our lives. I will turn no one away from this house. I want everyone who comes here to feel safe and secure and cared for—of any party or religion.

I'm having sad thoughts of poor Bulstrode—now so obviously sick in body and game in spirit. I am delighted to have this link with him through Mr. Philip Webb.

Wednesday 10th April

Crops—oats, barley, rye—growing fast and well and wild daffodils in the woods and leaves breaking on the trees and voices out of doors which are, to me, as much a sign of Spring as the return of nightingale and cuckoo. The cuckoo should be back in just over a week?

Thursday 11th April

That wretched little neglected Tom, whom I rescued from the mud several weeks ago, fell in the manure heap to-day. A miracle he was not smothered to death. His silly little mother scolded him and how was he to know, having climbed the fence, that it was not solid ground over the top? So I scolded her and told her she must keep him with her or she would lose her child and her job for negligence. He is only about two, and into everything, and exposed to ridicule since none admit to fathering him and his mother is probably unsure. I must try to keep her, for where else could she go? She belongs to Rockford. Might try to see if Madame Hubbard would have her, and the baby, two mornings a week, to teach her sewing and dressmaking. The work of the diary cannot be undone when it is wrong, as stitchery can! But—Harriet would be *very* much against her doing repairs and mending under *her* for the rest of the week!

Friday 12th April

Thinking much about and preparing for John H's coming tomorrow. I try to puzzle out what he is doing. I know he has his group in Portsmouth and a home of a sort there. I know he belongs to our group here. I know he is in touch with his Kingsbridge flock and has many friends in Lyme Regis and Plymouth. But—what of France, Amsterdam, the Hague? I know he has deep personal conflicts about the nature of priesthood and his own priest role, for he has this strong deep faith in the Spirit of God at work in each of us. I know politics bother him, too. It is hard for a young man to keep out of that world when two political parties are emerging closely bound to Catholic or Protestant religions.

I have decided I have no "religion", only a massive "faith"! I am totally loyal and yet guilty of "treason"!—I trust all men and have deep suspicions!

Saturday 13th April

After dark—late—I heard his voice in the servants' hall and he had come. With what control and dignity I could muster I went out—on some silly pretext—so that I might see him again. I love him so. Why, oh why do I see him like this, with all my own hope and faith and love and vision pinned on him? I know so little of him, really. Is he for or against the King? I know the standards of the Court appal him. Is he Calvinist?— NO! His humanity and sensuality are too live for that and he is positive, not negative. But is he Anglican? High? Or Protestant? I remember the chance thoughts he has dropped so many times of his ability to recognise and understand all positions. We are so at one in this. I am non-party—non-King— non-church—I am for Christ. (John Lisle's influence!—He was so strongly anti-Royalist, pro-Protestant. It is from his dogmatism that I recoil!) But this John, my John, John Hicks—the priest? Why was he priested? For power? For status? There is little of that in the lower branches of the Church and he seems to have no personal ambition. How does he see himself? What is he doing in Dorchester next week? Will there be any chance to see him alone? When he took my hand I longed for it never to be withdrawn. In a strange deep way our lives are bound together—How? Why?

Sunday 14th April

I was up early. Wandered through the kitchens, through the sheds and past the granary and the farm to the bluebell woods in Ellingham Drove. The others were all about, carrying flour to the bakery and letting the cows out. I had gathered a little bunch of periwinkle and I met him—coming back up the stream. He had been down to the river at Ibsley and a man down there had given him a salmon he had caught. He said he was a simple country lad. (James Dunne?)

We walked back together and he took my hand as he told me of his struggles to understand his role. He does not 'fit' the Church at any point, he says. They each wrangle over their tiny vision and lose the immensity in their short-sighted, self-centred peering, "A glass darkly."

A quiet meeting in the evening and he read the Dissenters' letter. I feel as if some of our group are a little suspicious of John's comings and goings. They do not doubt his sincerity, but are afraid of his forthright politics. But we country people are all afraid of taking a firm positive line, for always there are those who will rise up from the other side and betray and condemn us. The Dissenters beg us to keep firm and pray for them as they do for us.

Monday 15th April

John left—for Dorchester and then to Devon to his Kingsbridge group. He spoke more freely last night. Was ordained priest with great sincerity as a young man and is now lost, (his word), for he shrinks from the status and power thrust upon him and cannot find his place in the Church structure, in obedience to King, Court or Parliament when his allegiance is to God alone and the Spirit within him. Sensed something of self-centredness in him today—a pride (which he recognises) in his insights which he covers up, pushes under, and now cannot see. But I can, for my love for him is for his wholeness, not just his virtues. From what is he for ever running away? What is the search at the root of his restlessness?

Wednesday 17th April

Heavy rain all day and floods rising. Glad John got away before this downpour. Ford water deep by evening. Robert Whitaker called in on his way home. He spoke of death, having just been to the graveside of an old priest who had died in Ringwood. He mentioned the oration at the graveside, when it was suggested, that, just as we have faith in the resurrection of the dead, so we should have faith that we lived before this life began. The Word existed from the beginning with God and the Word returned to God after death. Could we not think this, therefore, also to be true of those of us who have faith in and follow the incarnate Word? Mystery and miracle. Is there no end to the explorations and revelations of the human mind? I pondered long, after Robert had left, and wondered whether John Hicks and I had met in a previous incarnation. Is that why our paths are now so entwined and my love for him (and his "feeling"—whatever it may be—for me) is so unshakeable. Or are our destinies bound together in the future? At death? After death? Beyond?

Thursday 18th April

Puzzling thoughts as we move towards the death and resurrection of Jesus in our daily prayers. My own thoughts and ideas were formed twenty and more years ago, when religious enthusiasm was high; now cynicism and science are all the rage and Catholics, Anglicans, non-conformers of all kinds, are setting their position in moulds, as the brick-makers make bricks and they will harden and be unyielding and forget they are of one clay. It is hard to follow my father faithfully. He was a staunch supporter of our Church at Ellingham, trying to save all that was best from the Reformation, and—I must support the family tradition. My life-time has been so full of change, and I understand the changes, yet feel no one understands *me*! Anything they say about me *could* be true!—Not proveable in law, but in gossip and surmise.

So—into these holy days.

Friday 19th April

I can't write. There's too much pain in it all. Not just the slow relentless pace of the last days of Jesus but the whole theme that has gone on, from that day to this, of the persecution and crucifixion of goodness; of the utter ridicule and blindness of the world to the struggle to find truth; of the confusion and garishness and superficiality of the human attempt to express beauty.

—And yet, there *are* the saints and martyrs, the thinkers

and seekers the poets and artists—still ready to die in their struggle to express the faith they hold. There is no end to that great stream of strugglers.

Saturday 20th April

I suppose this is the week when Catholics, Anglicans, Protestants are nearer sharing thoughts and outlooks than at any other time of the year. We all celebrate or consider the last week of Jesus' life and his death and resurrection. We all read the same passages in the Bible, and then we all go our separate ways to live out whatever our faith has revived in us through our meditations.

For many it is deep buried within, beyond expression or enactment. For others there is no deep understanding and others know not how to receive and for them, ritual and music and patterned words and lavish display is substituted and they try to feel as they should.

Between us all is a great gulf fixed. This must sadden God.

EASTER DAY 21st April

Easter Day at last! At last we can be happy and thankful again. I feel wearied by the strains and pains of these last days. They sang the Easter Anthem from the Book of Common Prayer so beautifully at Ellingham. I think we were all tired of the long days of Lent and the weight of the last week.

A lovely day of sunshine and racing clouds and new green on the trees and larks singing over the meadows. George Herbert's "Easter—Wings" came back to me—

> With thee
> O let me rise
> As larks, harmoniously,
> And sing this day thy victories:
> Then shall the fall further flight in me.

Dancing on Rockford Green in the evening. They always expect me to disapprove! I'm not that sort of Puritan.

61

Monday 22nd April

A very happy day!

The children brought me daffodils—the little wild Lent lilies—from the woods, anemones and celandine, and James Dunne brought tadpoles "to feed the ducks"! They may say he is simple, and so he is, but there is a great gentleness and sensitivity about him that is rare.

We had a large meal together—roast lamb—(unusual for us) and vegetable potage and pigeon pies and plovers' eggs, and early spring cabbage and mint jelly and roast goose and cranberry sauce, and steamed honey pudding and apple cake, and then they went off to games and dancing again at Rockford and some to Ringwood. (Do hope there are no cock-fights there. It doesn't stop though it is illegal. I should be sad if any of our men were caught there.)

Wednesday 24th April

A messenger on horseback brought the unbelievable news that Bridget is in London. She sailed in to Greenwich a week ago for Leonard* wanted books from Cambridge for Harvard University and also news of his family for he is not well and thinking of returning to England. She has come with a young student who is to go to Cambrdige to become a priest and has left little Biddy behind with her nurse. She tells me not to go to London to see her as she must attend to Leonard's affairs and then will come down here. Her journey took six stormy weeks, but all the ships and their crews and passengers arrived safely.

If she doesn't come and I get no further message I shall go up and stay with Elizabeth Hyde in Greenwich as I so much want to know why really, she has come home, why Leonard sent her for his books and what is this talk of his coming home. Her note was brief and I am anxious.

The men asked if they could take the waggon over to Downton this evening for the Cuckoo Festival. I was so over-joyed about Bridget that I said, if Ken would go, they could!—Though I haven't heard the cuckoo yet!

Thursday 25th April

Why did Bridget send me no letter? Did it go astray? Was her decision made very quickly? Why? I feel full of anxious questioning. I have had no letter from her for many weeks, and her last (early December) assured me that all was well—difficult, of course, but she was all right, and the University growing all the time.

Friday 26th April

Heard the cuckoo to-day! Am I getting a bit deaf?—When I told the others joyfully they each replied, "My lady, I heard it last week!" or "Madam, it has been around for days!" Never mind, my cuckoo lifted my spirits, as it does each year!

With Easter over, I must turn my mind to the new building as, any day now, Mr. Philip Webb will have the plans ready. Pilbeam asked today whether I had any more news, and said he is in touch with some men who will give us extra help when we need them. I think he is pleased that I am trusting him with the overseeing of it all. I gave him authority to cut more timber and tell Farmer Hackett to plough the fifteen acre field and sow rye or oats (if it is not too late) this year—far end—as much as he can fit in.

I seem to have much to plan and think about—many anxieties—Bridget, most of all, and then the building, and, as always, John Hicks—and the farm.

Saturday 27th April

A letter came from Mr. Webb the architect. He is coming on Wednesday or Thursday for my approval of plans and to work out the purchases and labour and timing. I must admit to being a bit awed by the whole thing, but it feels right to go ahead and I will not waver. It is for the growth of our community and to the glory of God and it must surely succeed.

So I gave all today to the building project. Went round woodstore and tool shed with Pilbeam, and made a list of what we have. Discussed the men he thinks will be useful and their wages. (We'll give as much as we can in food and produce, though it is not an easy time of the year for this.)*

63

Sunday 28th April

Sudden unexpected day of very heavy showers and then bursts of sunshine and then more squalls and very heavy rain. No one came to meeting from Ringwood or Gorley because of the rain, so we had prayers in the afternoon with just our household. I spoke to them on "A man's foes shall be they of his own household," for I am afraid our young people will give up searching for truth, being confused by the alternate apathy and fierce dogmatism in the Church and the political rift caused by Catholics and Protestants at war, and by the church's great wealth and power alongside the poverty and humility of our Lord. I want them to find their own truth based on the Man of the Gospels. God shone in him and through him and he said this was to be true for us also. But how can we hold to and live by and remember the good within when they never stop shouting about sin and evil and we must never stop repenting. If we are forgiven why keep up the moaning chorus? It seems morbid and faithless to me. John H. understands. "Miserable sinners"!—I can't be that whenever the Prayer Book suggests it—with the cuckoo singing and Easter still with us and baby mallards on the lake! though to-day's rain might drown them!

Monday 29th April

Found, in my anxious prayers this morning a lovely message from St. Paul—

"I, as a wise master-builder, have laid the foundation— and another buildeth thereon . . . Let every man take heed how he buildeth thereon . . . No other foundation can be laid than that which is laid, which is Jesus Christ . . .

. . . If any one builds on the foundation with gold, silver, precious stones, hay, wood, stubble . . . the Day will disclose it . . . fire will test what sort of work each one has done."

If then, I achieve this building, what future will be laid on these foundations. What sort of work will I, and those who follow me, be found to have done?

And I read on in Paul's letter and was awed and humbled by what he wrote in the verses that followed—Paul, Apollos, Cephas—Puritan, Anglican, Catholic—"all are yours; and you are Christ's; and Christ is God's.

Mr. Webb came yesterday evening and stayed the night. He has brought the plans and we went over them together in the evening, and I was pleased with them. He has included new kitchens and a new servants' hall and quarters, He is right. We shall need them, for there will be those who stay in the house, and they will all have servants to be housed. It is all larger, and therefore will be more costly than I had realised so we have cut out coach-house and stabling that he wanted. But I like Mr. Webb and we walked down Ellingham Drove together towards the church and he was very easy and courteous. He returned to Salisbury after noon and has left me to engage builders and the rest by mid-May. Pilbeam has contacted the Gorley blacksmith and found two brothers beyond Fritham who have a kiln and will supply all the bricks we want. Mr. Webb has a sister, married to a Fordingbridge lawyer, James Matthews, (Margaret and Robert know him well) and will stay with them, riding over here as often as necessary to keep things going. (He spoke of a wife who died some years ago, and two sons, but of no present wife.)

MAY

Wednesday 1st May

May Day! And games at Ibsley near Mockbeggar cross. There was Morris dancing and a fool and a hobby horse and a caravan of gypsies and a maypole and a crowd of singing boys with lute and tabor, and pedlars and carts from all round with laughing families and happy children. I could be (and probably am) condemned for being there or at least misunderstood, by many round, who know my devotion to our Lord, and my puritan and protestant views and contempt for the greed and wealth and pomp of the church. I should swing the pendulum right the other way, and condemn music and singing and dancing—so 'they' think. But, *no*!—Our Lord himself feasted and sang, and drank wine and mixed with the suspect and outcast and poor, and I feel no need to do otherwise. So, with Harriet, her little James, and many of my household I walked down to Mockbeggar in the evening to see the revellers, and I had given them a deer to roast on a spit—but the first slice of venison to give to whom I would!—I chose Betty Smithers. She is being so brave since her father died in January and I think should know why I chose to honour her. Her children were *very* proud! Cockfighting I fear at night and much drunkenness and that I can't approve.

Thursday 2nd May

Stiff to-day!—Because I danced with dear simple James Dunne last night!* The villagers tease him mercilessly, so I chose him to lead off with me. We did not do badly and I helped him keep time. We were applauded at the end, and were both pleased, and the children garlanded us with honeysuckle and flowers!—It was worth being stiff for all that. *But*—I was *Dancing* and this is disapproved by the *true* Puritans around for they see no difference between my giving encouragement to James and licentious, lewd dancing after

66

May Day drinking. *Why* these extremes? There is a middle way and I would tread it. (No one understood me when the King's head fell and I was *glad*, at the end of a superficial, selfish, irresponsible reign, and I *wept* at the King's death, and at John L's hatred and venomous attack on him and his part in his death. Relief and pain went together.) I cannot take sides. Neither can I change my loyalties from King to Parliament, from church to state, from Catholic to Protestant, as those do, who seek only for power and scurry, fawning, to be where power is—till they must fly for their lives, as Sir John did to Switzerland. No news from Bridget.

Friday 3rd May

Bridget's messenger at last. She cannot come down here for a few more weeks, and is not well. I must go to London. Not very easy, with Mr. Webb anxious to get on with the new wing, but even if things must be delayed, I must see Bridget. Sent the messenger back to tell her I will leave for Greenwich on Monday and arrive on Wednesday and stay for a week. Sent a message to Elizabeth Hyde as well, for she will make me welcome and our reunions are always good. The household were put out by my decision, but rallied round and busied themselves, for after tomorrow I do not want to ask much of them. Shall take Kenneth with me for the coach and he will select wagonners and a stable boy, and the horses. I have told little Katie Bolwell she can come with me, if her parents will let her. I have been training her as a lady's maid, and she has never been away from Ringwood, or into another household. She is timid and excited, and must wait till Sunday's conventicle to ask her parents; I'm sure they will agree.

Saturday 4th May

Balmy sunny day. Spent the morning with Harris planting and sowing. He is good and brought cuttings and seedlings of herbs and flowers. Trimmed the lavender hedge and clipped the rosemary and took new cuttings.

I packed the chest and selected the furniture and linen for London, and the men have the wagon ready for Monday.

Sunday 5th May

I went to Ellingham Church (painful duty, but Mr. Croft persuaded me as usual that for "the sake of the confused and weak people round" my example was "necessary"). More packing and then the Conventicle in the evening made it a busy day. "The Sabbath was made for man," Yes! I do not "work", and all my servants and household know this to be the Lord's Day, and a day of rest, and I expect no "work" from them. But I do not treat the day as a day of idleness and am at peace ordering my garden, tending my flowers and tidying my things. A day of rest and orderliness.

John Crofts led our meeting and preached on "our duty to God and our neighbour". I knew it was aimed at me and my reluctance to go to Ellingham. He only partly understands my determination to be free from priestly domination. (But he knows nothing of my love for John Hicks and the liberation that love has brought me.)

Monday 6th May

Set off for London before noon. Stopped for the night at St. Cross* and found it much the same. I always get a kindly welcome there for, although it is over twenty years ago, I had good friends in Winchester. Old Everett still there—very frail now and nearly blind. Katie Bolwell did very well and seemed reasonably at ease with the other servants.

Tuesday 7th May

Left St. Cross early as they asked me to call at Farnham Castle with a message to the Bishop and papers from the Dean.

Spring in the trees and hedges and fields as we journeyed eastwards and so arrived at Elizabeth's house. A tumultous welcome from all her children. Even the dogs welcomed me! Elizabeth has asked Bridget to stay here, too, but she was out when we arrived as she expected me tomorrow. Very tired. (So were the horses which we had changed at Farnham, and Ken will take these four back tomorrow and stay in Farnham with my waggon and coach until the 14th when I must return).

Just before dark I heard her coach in the yard and she came quickly to me. She was pale and thin and Elizabeth sent us food and wine to have together in my room so that we could talk freely. We watched the river which seemed fuller of ships than ever and the little one that had brought Bridget looked too frail for that long journey. I was very tired and so was Bridget so we slept soon—sooner than we wanted with so much to talk about. Bridget is not well.

Wednesday 8th May

Awoke and looked from my room over the Greenwich Observatory down on to the river. Much movement of tugs and flapping of canvas as a great East India Company ship moved into mid-stream to sail off on the tide, who knows where? A Dutch trawler followed her—going back to Holland I imagine. We were so transfixed by the river scene that we were nearly late for family prayers before breakfast. Bridget went out early. She is looking for a house in case Leonard leaves Harvard and returns to England*. What is worrying her? Leaving her daughter behind, I know, but more than that.

Ken, very thankfully, returned to Farnham (with young Philip who had never seen London or the river!) How Ken hates to leave the horses with anyone else!

This is a happy family, and they are a joy to stay with, though I can never discover who everyone is, for Elizabeth has several maids being tutored by her and Edward has naval cadets, often here waiting for their papers, and there are always cousins from the country, like me, with their staff and servants. It is all coming and going!

Thursday 9th May

A very full day. Caught the early tide and went with Bridget and Elizabeth by river to Westminster. I love that journey. Two young girls Elizabeth is training, Anne and Mabel, came too, and my Katie. Bought candles and a spinning wheel—the latter for Harriet and a little wooden doll for Katie. Shops were all bustle and the markets busy, but I missed the old Royal Exchange from the pre-Fire days, with its bookshops and apothecaries. Elizabeth and I loved our visits there together when we were first married, and John and I lived up here.

69

Went to a coffee-house in St. James's with Edward and his friends. Much gossip and talk of politics and trade, of religious dissent and unrest everywhere.

Back before dark—by the river again as lanterns were lighted and London's bells rang out at 6 p.m. Still signs of the Great Fire—charred timbers heaped up by the river and St. Paul's church still being demolished. They say Sir Christopher Wren's new building is going to be a very modern new design and he is determined it shall rise from the ruins and dominate London. I wonder what sort of worship will be carried on there in the coming years and centuries?

Friday 10th May

Bridget and I talked far into the night. She had a miscarriage on the boat. Leonard had sent her home when they knew she was pregnant as the spring is a time of much sickness and death in the New World. He insisted that Biddy should stay at home. She has a marvellousand devoted nurse. It was wise but sad and Bridget misses her so much. No wonder she is pale and unwell. Says she is recovering now. The speed of life in London is so different from the country and we seem always to be going to somewhere or something and others coming to us or going. Wore my new green taffeta gown. It was all right, but—so much expensive new fashion everywhere—so much jewellery! I feel it wrong to lavish so much on dress, and the strict Puritans we met and saw on the streets in their black and white and grey seemed to hold the truth about our faith as firmly as if they carried banners or shouted from pulpits that the pomp and wealth and display of court and church were a mockery of the quiet humble Spirit housed in our human bodies. Bridget laughed at me for there is no chance in New England to let your dress reveal your ideas! "Enough to have clothes to wear!" Bridget said!

So much to think over when I get home. Poor Bridget! Her future so unsure.

Saturday 11th May

Days too full to write this! I'm very tired, but it is worth it. So many old friends to visit, so much news to catch up on, of friends' children married, new children born and some old

70

friends now frail and ill and some have died. Little chance for much talk with Bridget. Had a cold, which was a nuisance—from the river, I suspect, or the general unfamiliar life and bustle of London. Not only from what I have seen, but from the way they all talk I find London a mixture of utterly sordid and noisy—the narrow streets, the smells, the noise, the quarrelling, fighting apprentices (scaring both horses and me!) and the markets and wharves—and also a strange gleaming beauty, with silver ripples on the Thames, the church bells, the ancient buildings and towers, and the fashionable pageantry and masques. I just feel confused and bewildered, though I am not new to this! Only out of touch these days, with no wish to belong to its gaudy, noisy, drab, materialistic society, with little space for quiet thought.

And I am troubled about Bridget who is cheerful with her friends and is obviously recovering but there is a great sadness and reserve there, and so little chance for us to talk together.

Sunday 12th May

I got up late and stayed away from church and was glad of that break in routine and no responsibility to be an "example" to others!

While they were all at church I found a lovely old lyric of Mr. Beaumont's and Mr. Fletcher's which brought back the London of my younger days. Very nostalgically, un-puritanically, surreptitiously, delightedly, I copied it into a back page of this diary.*

Elizabeth called musicians in to-day and we had lovely singing in the evening.

Monteverdi:—Beautiful setting of "Exulta Filia Sion," and madrigals—especially 'O mia bene', and 'Mia Vita' (Italian lost on me, of course!) She has a harpsichord and virginal and organ in her drawing-room and all the family are very musical. Her two sons sang tenor and bass, and Charles, the tenor, is a gorgeous boy with such a lovely voice. All their servants gathered at the door to listen. It calmed my con-fusion of yesterday. Who would have thought I, who knew London so well twenty years ago, would have been so bewildered by it all? Partly the shock of Bridget's story, I suppose, and having a cold.

71

Monday 13th May

Bridget was very tearful last night. The music had upset her and the coffee house we went to in St. James; even the walk in the King's new park at St. James's failed to calm her. She told me a little of why. But I am sure it is mostly that she has done too much after the long, anxious, journey, and then her miscarriage, and now more anxiety about telling Leonard and getting all his requests satisfied—house, books etc. The young man, Timothy Shuttleworth, who came with her is in Cambridge and responsible for the latter.

It is the contrast with her New England life that has hit her hard. She is not such a strict Puritan at heart. (How could a daughter of such parents be!) She has conformed as a loyal wife to Leonard, and New England has not the varied social pressures that London offers and those around her there are strict conformers to their nonconformity! "I loved the music!" She said, and "The freedom of speech in that coffee house!" and "All that money on parks and gardens! Ours is all in books and oats and rye and guns!" I can understand her confusion. Dear Bridget! I have let Katie look after Bridget's things. She was very sweet and helpful. Leonard is having a very hard time at Harvard—unpopular and there are very few new students.

Tuesday 14th May

Packing up to-day, as Kenneth will want an early start tomorrow. He is always anxious to pick up 'his' horses again, and anxious to return others safely. Bridget in Shoreditch but will come over in the morning. I ache for her in all her hardships which are only, little by little, coming to light. All Leonard's visions and hopes and plans of the last three years seem dashed and Bridget seems to get the brunt of his harshness and unreasonableness—and now has to return to him without the son he longs for.

Bridget is in regular touch with Tryphena. My poor little Tryphena! She is still in Wales with the impossible Lloyd, and Bridget is urging her to leave him and join her in New England and start a new life. But with Leonard's ill-health and their now uncertain future it would be another foolishness. But I am thankful Bridget and Tryphena write regularly. Bridget says that if Tryphena does decide to leave Lloyd and join her she has made her promise to come and see me before she leaves the country. Five years since she ran away. Unbelievable. Meeting again would be difficult, but how I long to see her. She is well, Bridget says, but very poor.

Wednesday 15th May

Kenneth arrived last night and loaded the waggon and coach. Again, the Bishop's horses, so Ken fussing and anxious to get to Farnham. Bridget arrived to see me off. She expects to be in London until July but will come and stay at Moyles Court for a week or two soon, to see Margaret and Robert and other Forest friends. Journey straightforward and Bishop Morley welcoming, but "busy". (Finds me a problem, I suspect.) Joined his household for evening prayers in his chapel. Solemn. Beautiful. But he blessed me with such anxious fervour that I felt he was offering to my Lord a very problem person! I bent to kiss his ring as he expected, but I only bent, and gave no kiss, and he looked at me with what I felt was supposed to be reproof, but I saw a spark of understanding!! Was that possible?? He has always been an enigma—as I have!

I was given supper in my room and seen courteously to bed by his women servants, and saw him no more. The Palace must be, I suppose, half hostelry, and I, as wife of Sir John, though a decade ago, suspect!—But—that spark of understanding in chapel?? (I think I was pushed off to my room early as the Bishop of Bath and Wells and Sir Isaac Newton are coming here tomorrow.)

Thursday 16th May

Set off early in the morning for Winchester. Stayed again at St. Cross, and the brothers welcomed me so graciously. Glad I decided to go straight home tomorrow and not call at Alresford and Cheriton. I am tired and feel so much is happening at Moyles Court, and I should be there.

Friday 17th May

Back home! A good London visit, but I am a country woman and Moyles Court is my home and my delight and the household, every one of them, very dear. Good to be back and pick up the threads of home again. Pilbeam has done well, and has a good team of labourers ready. Mr. Webb came over while I was away and told Pilbeam just how it was to go, where materials should be stored, and the part he was to play. Perhaps it was as well that I was away and they could work closely together. Pilbeam thrives on responsibility and seemed confident, though he has recently had two falls, one from a tree and one from a horse and his back is very painful. Great piles of brick and timber everywhere and steady work seems already under way.

Wish John Hicks were nearer. He must be in Kingsbridge or Stoke Damerel or somewhere in Devon, which all seems very far away.

Saturday 18th May

The nightingale sang all night and there was a near full moon, and I went to the window to listen. It was away in the bushes on the hill towards Whitefield, and I watched the deer grazing and moving stealthily in the mist. Very quiet till the nightingale, unashamed, broke the stillness. London's noise and bustle and the river full of traffic seemed so far away—yet under the same moon!

Busy, contented day! Much laundry blowing in the wind! Much tidying up to do and much unpacking, and my little gifts to distribute. Tidying up needed of my mind and spirit, too. There have been so many distractions and perplexities!

Rev. Croft came in the evening ready for our early morning meeting. It will be good to see them all again, and Katie Bolwell very excited. I shall let her go home until Tuesday. Rev. Croft interested in all I had to tell him, but I had none of the news he really wanted—of the Whitechapel conventicle, the King's attitude to Catholics, Protestants, the gossip about succession, the Dutch etc! He wasn't very interested in Bridget and the New World! I felt I badly disappointed him with my absorbtion in family and friends, but he was kind and attentive.

Sunday 19th May

Happy morning meeting! I had a warm welcome, and the Bolwells overjoyed to see Katie back again. They took her home after meeting and I dutifully went with the others to Ellingham. I am much happier in my grey and white-trimmed worsted gown than trying to match the finery of London.

Monday 20th May

A letter from Bridget who leaves London for Moyles Court to-day. She has received disturbing news from her husband. He has had two minor heart attacks and she must go back to Harvard next month—not at the end of July as I had hoped. Dear Bridget, how hard her life is being and Leonard Hoar a strange man—all brains and learning. No one thought, least of all Bridget, that she would live in the New World and she is finding life very strange and difficult. It is two years now since he was made President—almost immediately after his course of sermons in Massachusetts—soon after he returned with his Cambridge M.D. It is proving an unpopular appointment with the students and Leonard's quick temper flares up with them—and her. She speaks guardedly but often, about one Hezekiah Usher, a staunch protestant with whom she says she "feels freer" and "has much sympathy".* He seems to give her the companionship that Leonard cannot give. Leonard says that little Biddy is well and already trying to read.

Tuesday 21st May

Of course I want Bridget here, but it is sooner than I expected and I would not have gone to London if I had known I would be seeing her so soon. I really need more time to get ready for her.

No more writing! I must get quiet and still and strong and ready for tomorrow.

Wednesday 22nd May

Late in the evening Bridget's coach arrived. Wonderful to have her here and we shall have time together at last. She is tired, of course, but days of quiet here will help and she says she has found a London house if it becomes necessary, and has done most of the things Leonard asked regarding books and University needs. I sent her to bed early, though I was longing to talk. There will be time in the coming days and I must not rush her. She was very sound asleep when I joined her.

Thursday 23rd May

The footings are going on well for the New Wing. It is all pegged out and bricks arrive daily and are stacked for laying and the carpenters are sorting and sawing and measuring.

I took Bridget out to dig a sod so that she could feel she had contributed to the building, and she met the men and spoke to them all graciously. She was always like that and always concerned for people, even as a very little girl. Pilbeam is doing well and says he has found plenty of willing helpers from the estate, who for food and ale and some of our own forest rights and produce will work willingly. Pilbeam is friendly with Col. Pennruddock's head forester at Hale!— Awkward coincidence and I hope no more trouble brews up from that old dispute.

Turned the old coach house over to the carpenters and stone-masons as their workshop. The coach and hay wain can stay out for the summer now and the little carriage.

Friday 24th May

My birthday.

Happy walk with Bridget, over the ford and up to the Cuckoo pines and we sat on its roots and looked out to Badbury Rings and heard the bells at Fordingbridge Church. Every moment with her is precious. My thoughts fly so far and I must let her go, sadly, on their wings!—But I know too, that this time she will never return. So many leave our troubled country and no news returns. On the way back we watched fish in the stream and a newt clambering up the bank. Bridget rooted up a last year's acorn from the moss where we were sitting; it had pushed down a small strong root and the shell had cracked and germinated. We planted it, ceremonially together and B. said, "Grow now, little New Forest tree till the birds fly home and nest in your branches!"* It said much to us both—a symbol of our Moyles Court days and our whole community here—brief, fleeting, but good and part of a strange, unknown, eternal pattern—Kings and commoners, all a part—and an oak tree to cement the whole. I shall watch that spot and guard that little shoot. A great tree could be there three hundred years ahead. Watched nuthatches and a tree-creeper busy on a tree-trunk and the kingfisher shot down-stream—and Bridget part of the fringe of the world.*

Saturday 25th May

Too busy to write! My morning quiet is altogether given to prayers and thoughts. It is more important to still my soul and feel close to the Spirit of God than scribble here, and there's so much going on! Also, I think, with Bridget's companionship (and I'm getting to know and respect this young, matured, married daughter more and more) I have no need to pour out lonely discourses here! She listens to me, and is very understanding, but she has become a very strict Puritan since living in Boston and they seem very united in their acceptance of rigid rules. (They are fined if they do not attend their meetinghouse on Sunday.)

Sunday 26th May

Bees swarmed in early evening. So much silly shouting and running around that I thought we would lose them. But Harriet drove the staff all inside, waving her broom and scolding, and I went with Pat, Ken Buckton and Rev. John Crofts (!) and the new rush skep and sacks and we got them safely. Better than last year when we lost them and had bad weather for bees, so little honey—and little mead for Christmas. Bees are no respecters of the sabbath, and evensong was out of the question. Morning as usual. Warm, beautiful spring days and early summer now and the garden lovely with gilliflowers and forget-me-nots and stocks and lupins. Glad Bridget is seeing an English spring again. "It is so quiet and orderly and gracious!" She said. And my mind teeming!!

She has gone over to Fordingbridge for two nights, and has decided not to go back to London till after next week-end, now that her plans are so changed. (No need to settle about a house.)

77

Monday 27th May

Bridget has given me a list of things she hopes to take back with her. I am copying it here as I'm sure to lose the list she gave me:

    Pins and Needles
    Kettle. Frying Pan. Tankards. Bowls
    Little pots and jars
    Candles. Candlesticks
    Nails. Leather. Bellows. Spades. Hoe
    Linen. Buckram. Lace
    Scissors. Shears
    Barrels for packing—useful when emptied
    Garden flower seeds
    A toy for Biddy

Asked Pilbeam to get three barrels in three sizes from the cooper and arrange for hinged lids so they can use them for chests. Ordered nails, spade, shears and hoe from Gorley blacksmith, and some iron brackets. How can I find garden seeds in May?! The carpenter is carving a doll and a horse for my granddaughter.

Whitsun revels in Ringwood. When Bridget got back she was a little shocked when I asked if she would like a drive round to watch the Morris men. She is now a much stricter Puritan than her mother!—The effect of the Boston group? Obviously the pattern of the Pilgrim Fathers has influenced them all in the last fifty years. They left this country to preserve their strict ideas and do not live, as we do, surrounded by other ways of living.

Tuesday 28th May

Turned out chests and cupboards to find things for Bridget. Plenty of linen and cloth and strong hessian she can have. Made a pile for her to sort out and sent a message to the tinkers to bring their things up here for her to see when she gets back tomorrow. Some of the children's clothes will be useful for her, too. What memories in those little gowns and pinafores and pantaloons!

Wednesday 29th May

Flags flying to-day for the King's birthday and I let Pilbeam share a new barrel of ale with the workmen to celebrate. He agreed it would be wise diplomacy! The place seems full of people—carpenters, stone-masons, blacksmiths, apprentices, assistants—and noise! And dust! Sawing! Hammering! Chipping!—Dragging planks and beams, and piling up bricks. I can see it will be worse before it is better and am thankful for Mr. Webb. No wonder Bulstrode was so emphatic that I needed a good architect and how right he was.

The tinker and his wife came and Bridget bought several things from them.

Thurday 30th May

Was horrified to-day when Harriet and two of the builders came to me to say the men (Barter and Dowding) whom Harriet suspected of stealing my linen in January had turned up again to haul and cut timber for the new wing. Pilbeam took them on as haulers from Col. Penruddock at Hale. I felt there might be trouble from Hale but had never thought those two rascals would turn up again in these parts. I warned Pilbeam to go carefully with them but found Harriet had already told him she would never allow them in or near the house or laundry or bakery or kitchen and would use the whip if they came near! Oh, Harriet!!

Can't understand John Penruddock employing those two again. In fact I don't believe he did and expect they lied to get this job, pretending they had only just left his service.

Mr. Webb called in briefly, but I missed him. He saw Pilbeam.

Friday 31st May

A big dinner party to-night for Bridget with Margaret and Robert and the four from Fritham, John and Catherine from Dibden and the Souths and Rev. Hobson: (Wife in bed with much coughing and sickness.) In spite of the trouble yesterday of Barter and Dowding, the kitchen stopped gossiping and got ahead with preparations and we spent the day preparing the hall for the evening. It looked lovely. We don't often, nowadays, prepare for such occasions. Bridget wore grey taffeta and Beconshaw lace and looked so pretty now that colour is returning to her cheeks. I shall see little more of her after Monday.

JUNE

Saturday 1st June

Packed the barrels and chests with Bridget's things for London. She may sail from Greenwich or may go down to Plymouth and join a boat there. It seems best to get everything to London since the coach will take her anyway, and if the waggon goes as well they will be well protected on the journey. So—soon I must say goodbye to her again.

Sunday 2nd June

Bridget came to meeting in the morning and several friends came out to say goodbye to her, and Margaret brought the children to meeting for the first time. (She stayed here last night and Robert, of course, went back for his Fordingbridge congregation.)

It is not often, for me, such a "family"—*real* family—gathering. I prayed hard fom my two daughters—so different in temperament, and with such different domestic problems. Bridget reminds me of her father often, and Margaret is meek and submissive like my mother. I prayed for Tryphena and Ann and wished they too could have been with us—and my sons.

Monday 3rd June

Bridget left for London, and I am left with aching heart. The coach left by mid-morning with the waggon loaded too. They will travel together to Winchester and then the coach, being quicker, will carry on with only the coachmen. They are safer in the forest travelling together, as there are vagabonds and thieves round Cadnam and the Rufus stone.

Margaret and the children went home and Harriet, knowing my heavy heart came constantly to ask me unnecessary questions about linen, and left-over food from the party, and to tell me gossip about Phyllis's latest affairs and James Dunne having only just realised that all kittens are born blind, and don't become blind cats!! She is so good to me; her endless prattle to distract me is sensitive and thoughtful. We went out to pick roses together and I felt better and knew life would go on for each of us in our own ways to the fulfilling of our destinies.

Tuesday 4th June

My thoughts of Bridget and her future had to be pushed behind to-day and give way to the building. The men have spent two days carting bricks over to the site and have put them all in the wrong place—where the carpenters want the timber. Pilbeam asked me to come out and speak to the men as Mr. Webb will not be back before Thursday. I was shocked. They are a rough, uncouth gang, and I hardly knew what to say, except that there would be no pay for those who were brawling and fighting and there were many others in the Forest who would be glad to work and I would give orders that they should be thrashed if they would not do as Pilbeam ordered, and that he was in charge, and that there were stocks in Ibsley village for thieves and disturbers of the peace and the local constable was a friend and frequent visitor to the house. They were quiet when I finished and I went quickly back into the house, hoping I had spoken enough and rightly, but unsure. Pilbeam came to me in the evening and said, "Thank you, Madam. It seems alright now. The craftsmen have built a shed to work in, and the bricks are now stacked alright, and the footings ready for Mr. Webb." "They know you are their master, Madam!" Harriet said. She had missed nothing of course!

Wednesday 5th June

Barter and Dowding have disappeared!—At least they have not been seen here since yesterday morning. (They missed my harangue!) I am relieved, for whether Harriet is right about them or not there was suspicion about, that might easily have caused trouble.

A day of drizzling rain. It will do the garden good and I thought yesterday how lovely it was looking, with roses and snapdragon and big yellow daisies and delphiniums and Canterbury bells and poppies and cornflower and sweet williams. My herb garden will be glad of rain. I miss old Smithers! He loved to walk round the garden with me in the summer and talk about plants and he knew a lot about old herbal remedies and wizard's potions. The vegetable garden is full of new growth—peas, beans, lettuce and spinach, carrots—all growing fast.

Thursday 6th June

Mr. Webb here for the day. I was thankful. He came to see me before he left and says all is going well, and the bricklayers will go hard ahead now and I shall begin soon to see walls rising. Pilbeam had told him about the problem with the men and he had called them all together and "made it clear" what would happen if they were troublemakers. "I'm sure it will be all right now there is real progress beginning and something to see for their efforts," he said. He will be back again on Monday. I like him and was very reassured by his visit.

Friday 7th June

I seem to have had no time for my family and household this week! It has been all building and builders!—Much more restless than our usual daily round!

Barter and Dowding have been caught and are to go before the court, but no one knows why. Needless to say, Harriet heard it!

Still drizzling rain.

Saturday 8th June

Barter and Dowding up before Col. Penruddock to-day for many offences.

They were finally brought to book by a farmer near Ringwood forest who caught them rolling a barrel of his cider—stamped with his brother's name from Somerset!—down the hill near Udden's Cross. Harriet had already told some local soldiers, billeted at Hale, that she hoped her mistress's linen would be found for she would recognise the lace on it wherever it turned up in the world. Faithful, loyal

Harriet, but she told the soldiers to look for it in Penruddock's barns—which was unfortunate, for the less traffic there is between Moyles Court and Hale Park the better under the circumstances!—But—too late now to lie low and say nothing! I'm glad they won't be looking for work here any more.

Sunday 9th June

Last week was not easy and I was thankful for a sabbath and John Crofts here for our evening meeting. I lived last week on surface feelings and turbulent events and even my morning's peace never brought the calm and quiet I need for my spirit and awareness of God's control. But what Rev. Crofts said was helpful and strengthening. His text: "This people honour me with their lips but their hearts are far from me". (Me, this week!) He spoke of magic, witchcraft, science, astrology, prophecy, of our rejection of a miracle of transubstantiation in the mass and of the priests' fear of secular magic that would undermine their authority. He spoke of the true insights of astrology and prophesy which point to God's Laws being revealed to us individually. (I thought of Mr. Lilly's almanacs and his prophetic gifts.) "The Bible is not just historic, it is your place of revelation and insight . . . To you is revealed the mystery—not just to kings, priests and lawyers . . . Your own insights will free you from the rule of this world if you read in prayer and humility . . . Study your Bible."

The discussion after was lively and spirit-filled. Mr. Bolwell spoke of Jesus reading a prophecy of Isaiah, seeing it as relating to himself, closing the book and sitting down. Jesus interpreted it for himself—as we can do to-day. All this soothed my unrest.

Monday 10th June

Mr. Webb here, but only briefly and mostly with the carpenters and stone-masons.

Oh dear! I must keep my head in all this. During family prayers I heard someone snuffling and gulping by the door and knew it was weeping. Went out after to the courtyard and found Phyllis, red-eyed and wretched. She is pregnant, silly girl, and dare not tell her father. By "one of these new men," she said. "I've tried to stop it," she said. Poor silly child! I told her she must find Ken and tell him. (She was afraid of a thrashing—rightly, I imagine.) We went together and found him in the stables. I waited in the doorway while Phyllis told him. He was ready to turn on her in fury, but in turning, saw me outside. "My Lady, what can a man do with a daughter like this?" he said. I said, "God alone knows, Ken, except that you must stand by her for Christ's sake." Phyllis's defiance broke down and she wept again. I sent her back to her work and stayed and talked to Ken, until he was calmer. Life went on, and I was thankful that Mr. Webb was about, keeping peace at the building end. Very tired by evening and the news of Phyllis causing gossip all round. "Of course, Madam!" was Harriet's comment.

Tuesday 11th June

Phyllis now back to her insolent, loud-voiced self. I took her aside and told her I would help her if she needed me and would show some remorse for her condition. She misses a mother and Ken's wife Joanne is not much older than she, and no doubt finds her in the way at their cottage, and, anyway, she has two very small children to care for. One can see reasons for Phyllis being as she is, but not excuses. "I will be alright, Madam. Never fear! I have plans for the child." I fear what these plans may be and must keep an eye on her. Difficult, as she works in the laundry and I cannot often go there. Jean must let me know if she is unhappy about the girl. I must be in authority over this, for the girl would be flogged to death if she had not the support of being in our household. The country folk are ready to condemn her, and yet the country lads and lasses, (and the old ones were young once!) have gone these ways since time began. I cannot condemn Phyllis when the stories of the King and his Court are more licentious than any we can offer here and they are called our leaders.

Wednesday 12th June

I heard a horseman gallop into the courtyard as I watched the builders this morning. Phyllis hurried out, "Madam, madam, it's Mr. Hicks!" By evening he had gone. I am left, proud, perplexed, confused. "May I see you alone?" He said. I called for cider and bread and cheese and meat for him, and gave orders that we should be alone in the back parlour and undisturbed. We were there from noon until early evening and he needed me, used me, to pour out the anguish and struggle of his life, his ambition, the reasons for his restlessness. "Who else can I safely share this with?" He said. "These thoughts, if I really bring them to action, would have me hung, drawn and quartered. I do not fear death, but I need my life, to give it in the service of the poor, the labourer, and the simple, voiceless people of the land who struggle as slaves under the feet and will and dominion of King, Parliament, Church, landowner—the rich, who have so much, indeed *all*, and hold it only through the services of the poor . . . Christ is meaningless to them, and the church whose servant I was ordained to be is merely a worldly law and authority which holds them down in guilt and fear and subservience" . . . "I owe allegiance to no man, but only to my God, through Christ" . . . "How must I live this?" . . .

Thursday 13th June

Events of these days must go unrecorded as I try to write what John poured out to me yesterday. There was so much more than I can record. He said, "The Revolution, the Civil War, the Commonwealth!—It was to liberate the poor from the stranglehold of Church and State. Look at things! King, Parliament, Bishops are in full authority again; a yeoman middle-class are sharing the power, enclosing more and more land, hedging in their new property, increasing their wealth, and the common people, the poor, who should be allowed freely to till the common land and heath and forest, are poorer still, despised, rejected, treated as scum. If they work for their lords and are paid a miserable wage this makes them more despised than when they slaved for feudal lords with at least some reciprocal return in protection and food from the land. What can their miserable "pay" give them, but increase their poverty and insecurity?" On and on he went. "I will give my life for the poor—those who live in hovels in the forests and on common land, who have so little, and no hope. These are the ones my Lord came to uphold: I cannot uphold the authority of the church, with its wealth and distortion . . .

"Oh Dame Alice, dear loyal friend, can you stand by me as I go hither and thither, defying the authority I was ordained to serve, a soldier in a 'New Model Army' of Christ's for the poor and destitute?" He spoke of his family and upbringing in Yorkshire. (His grandfather was a Plymouth ship-owner and his grandmother, a "Cornish woman", "one of the poor"; that's where his links with Cornwall, Stoke Damerel and Saltash began.) He has been reading much from the prophet Isaiah, and where Jesus reads from Isaiah in the Gospel about setting free the oppressed, and preaching good things to the poor. "We are traitors to the Gospel," he said. "How can I accept the authority of the priesthood when my Master accepted authority only from the Spirit within him?" He was in real anguish. "My visits to France, to Holland, to Lyme, are all to do with this. There are others like me who support the still hopelessly down-trodden, the vagrants, the pedlars and the beggars, the folk living in shacks and hovels and cottages on the common lands. They need someone to speak for them. And the urban poor too . . ., I would be one of them, speak for them, help them to rise up and defeat their oppressors." "Thirty years ago," he said, "I believe they had much support from the soldiers after the Civil War, but apathy has set in again and laws have been passed to quell them and keep them subservient, and power and wealth is again held tightly in the grip of King, Parliament and Church . . ."

Saturday 15th June

I have only recorded a fraction of all he said, but I understood and felt so proud that he could confide in me. I felt afraid for him, too, for although he is gentle and in many ways timid and lacking in confidence, when he feels strongly he can speak forcefully and hastily.

As a boy of sixteen he was sent to an uncle in Somerset before going to study in Dublin. He stopped near London and by chance worked for two weeks in Walton-on-Thames with Gerrard Winstanley, a "Digger". I remember Bulstrode speaking of Diggers. They wanted a world free of land-ownership, without money, where none were high or low.

Marvellous idea, but no chance of its being workable. "This is why I studied hard in Dublin. This is why I became a priest. This is why it is hard now to be a priest."

"Forgive me," he said, as he left, "This is how I am, and I want you to know, for I shall give my life, and probably die for this cause."

Sunday 16th June

All last week's diary given to John's swift visit on Wednesday. Life has gone on at Moyles Court without me!—Very good for me to find I was not necessary to its life!—I wandered about in a dream, much in the garden and orchard,—though it has been showery with only bursts of June sunshine. Mr. Webb was right, and the new wing is raising itself above the ground—somehow looking smaller as it gets bigger!

I have marvelled at the relevance of last Sunday's meeting and Mr. Croft's words and what folk said after. John H. actually quoted the same prophesy that Mr. Bolwell spoke about. And John 'prophesied' his own life and death and I have felt in me this week the truth of my own insights and a clarity of seeing that I never knew when I looked to priests—or my husband—as interpreters and intermediaries for me. I have an immense feeling of Truth, stirring, seething in the land, from King's Court to Moyles Court,—of a liberation of the spirit of man from some age-old tyranny, from shackles and stocks of the past. Phyllis, John Hicks, the new wing—everything is rising, climbing up to express new freedom, new ideas, new visions. Science, mathematics—these new approved studies allow the learned to accept and explore magic, astrology, witchcraft and the old lore and runes that the common people have known for generations.

Monday 17th June

There seemed fewer men about the building and I wondered why. Sent for Pilbeam and heard that Mr. Webb had told him to send away the six unskilled men he had called in for the haulage of materials, timbers and bricks and sand and things, as their rough manual work was finished. They left on Friday and I am glad. They were ruffians and strangers and thieves and disrupted our lives. I wonder if I would have started this building if I had realised how much upheaval there would be. I saw this morning that they have felled a larch tree that had been so lovely in early spring and have destroyed a bluebell patch of woodland where I had often stood to marvel. Building is fasionable now. Have I been caught in a public wave of prosperity? Aftermath of Plague and Fire and War? Restoration of, not only the Monarchy, but our more stable way of life? But I build this for a purpose—the hospitality that Moyles Court can offer to those searching for freedom and peace—to the John Hicks of this world—a refuge and a retreat.

Tuesday 18th June

Yesterday's thought, that I had perhaps been caught in the wave of prosperity that has undoubtedly followed the Restoration, had a bad knock this morning. The King is calling for new taxes "for the navy", he says, but for the Court, I suspect. And Mr. Webb is needing a substantial amount of money for the building and already I have paid out more than I had foreseen. Prices are going up all the time, and there is no going back for me now. I spent part of to-day anxiously looking at the books where I record my accounts. I so much want to do this all with Beconshaw money, but fear it will not be possible, and then John is sure to hear at Dibden and he will resent it.

The feeling for rebuilding and a new start has seeped through from London to the country for our families and friends go to and fro so much and we are affected.

There is new building or restoration and repairs going on in so many of the family houses around.

No news from Bridget.

Friday 21st June

All my spare thoughts in the last few days have been on money. How I hate it!—Because I hate the confused thoughts that go with it. It is my inheritance and on trust and a responsibility. But it is a material possession and, as such, not mine, but loaned to me for wise use by my God. But why should I have so much and live so close to so many who have so little, or nothing? Generosity cannot be measured by how much you give, but by how much is left after giving. Meanness is measured not by giving, but the amount withheld. I have so much and it worries me. Perhaps when all these accounts are settled and we are using the new wing I will feel better—being then both richer in possessions and poorer in money. Ken's cottage roof is leaking and will have to be mended this summer, but we may have all we need to do it on the estate and with our forest timber rights. (Unless the King takes those away!).

Saturday 22nd June

A letter from Bridget! She was to sail from Greenwich yesterday for Dartmouth and then to Plymouth and then across the world. She says, "Forgive me that I have seemed so detached and occupied with my own anxieties. I feel a foreigner on English soil for both my world and yours change so fast these days; I cannot grow two ways at once and my heart is in my little daughter's world. But I found peace and strength in your world at Moyles Court and cherish every memory. Build well above the sod I dug, and guard the little birthday oak I planted for you by the stream". Very dear Bridget—I cannot miss her for we are too close for distance to separate us—"We live in one another still." (John Hicks Jan.20)

Sunday 23rd June

Once again grateful for the companionship and peace of our group. Once again shocked—I have to hold back *tears*!—by the sham of Ellingham. But the meeting was good. Two things stand out for me there—1) The silent praying, when I, who so love words, find depths of peace beyond them, 2) The discussions that happen so freely after the sermon, for, if the preacher is shallow or short or uninspired, the thoughts of even our humblest members, enrich and enlighten us, and we share ourselves with each other in ways that can never come about in dairy or kitchen, in hall or closet. It all depends on trust.

But Ellingham! I keep trying to escape into my own thoughts and yet get dragged back to being "Mrs. Lisle" in the "Moyles Court pew", looking down on them all, while in our conventicle, though they may call me "Dame Alice", I look up, to them, and my Lord. (Lord God—not Sir John!—Even if it is because of him I have this title!)

Monday 24th June

Monday—three days since Bridget left. I sent the boys over to fish at Bicton Mill and leave Bridget's letter with Margaret so that they would know she had gone. The boys came back in the evening with a good catch, but they said Margaret and Robert were "away for a few days"—the children still there. Where have they gone, I wonder?

Tuesday 25th June

Phoebe's husband rode over from Fordingbridge this morning with a note from Margaret. She and Robert heard from Bridget on Saturday, as I did, and they left for Dartmouth yesterday morning hoping to be in time to see her. She will surely come ashore for some hours for they will pick up food and water and passengers there, and then have to wait for the tide to lift them on their way. Oh, I hope they don't miss her! Robert has a cousin in Lyme and many friends, mostly non-conforming ministers, on the road west. They must have made a very sudden decision—unlike Robert who is so calculating and cool.

Wednesday 26th June

Oh, Bridget, what awaits you? I cannot help but miss her, for we have been closer and warmer and more understanding since she came home than ever before in her life. Sorrow and pain are the things that make up growth, help us to see ourselves and then understand others more, and she is now having to bear in her miscarriage, as I did in mine, much sorrow and pain.

Thursday 27th June

So often I feel a fool! Why can I not, at my age, give up the struggle to find my own way and live as I feel right? Why am I never content to be obedient and conform and accept authority? How easy to be a Catholic!—Give up and accept the decisions of others and just obey! It is not that I feel I know better than they, but nothing rings true unless it comes from within me, confirming, not just conforming. Yet this deep sort of stubbornness makes me often feel a fool, a heretic, fit only to be burnt at the stake like other 'suspects', or excommuni-

91

cated, or even executed for treason, rejected, feared. Mr. Lilly has said this is my destiny, for my astrological sign is Gemini and I must therefore always see two ways,—the Janus—always restless unless both sides are understood. Other people fear this in me for I see the other side, the dark side, of themselves, of which they are so often afraid. That is why it was so very special for me that John H. could trust himself to me.

Was it Luther who said, "Here I stand, so help me God, I can no other" . . .? I can say that from the heart as well.

Friday 28th June

Will Margaret and Robert get back to-day? Will they find her? When will they come and let me know? If they don't get home until tomorrow they will not have time to see me before Monday. I must be patient.

Saturday 29th June

They found her.!

Margaret called in on her way to Ringwood market to tell me about their journey and Bridget's departure. They got back at mid-day to-day, having had two nights with friends of Robert's each way—and they saw her. (It was so good of Robert to go!—The kindest, most helpful thing I have ever known him to do, for Margaret or our family, and I am grateful.) Bridget was astonished and delighted. They met her by the Customs' house, so easily, on Wednesday—the day they arrived. Bridget's boat reached Dartmouth on Tuesday, having called in at Southampton on Sunday. John had sailed round from Lymington to see her leave and followed her down the Solent. She left Dartmouth on the full tide on Thursday morning. Bridget took them aboard to see round. She seemed a "sturdy, tidy, little ship" and the captain a "stocky, silent, sailor," Robert said, but "experienced" and well used to the Atlantic crossing. They had a meal together at a Dartmouth tavern near the quay before she sailed. There were three other women passengers, only one of whom had been to New England before, older than her, with a boy of eight, but Margaret said they seemed friendly and the two young ones were very frightened. Bridget would help them.

92

Sunday 30th June

A much needed, peaceful Sunday and everyone so full of sympathy and understanding of Bridget's departure. Reason tells me that she and Leonard could return to England, especially if Leonard has to resign and is unwell. But intuition tells me that they will not return and I shall not see Bridget again. Reason is one-legged and intuition one-winged!—We sang the 23rd Psalm—it carries truth beyond reason, beyond intuition—and I will fear no evil—for goodness and mercy will follow me and Bridget all the days of our lives, whatever the enemies around us may do.

JULY

Monday 1st July

Got down to business again with a new week, and was excited to see the carpenters and stone-masons and bricklayers all working together to put up the scaffolding for the next storey. I think they are now enjoying working together and seeing their separate skills combining. I study the plans inside now, and am beginning to visualise it all. There is a large hall downstairs with a gallery at one end, so that the hall can be a place for any kind of meeting we may want, or for a dining hall, and the gallery can be used by those caring for young children, free to come and go, or for music, or readings—many, many thing. The kitchens are very modern—the Gorley blacksmith has been helping with the new kitchens at Breamore House, and is full of their new spits and bread oven.

Tuesday 2nd July

Several times lately I have met, above Ibsley, crossing the moors at the place we call Whitefield (because the gravel pushes through, white and ivory, and shines by moonlight), the son of a cottager I hardly know, from near Gorley. He has just returned from France and is now a tall, stiking young man. He had stood aside to let me pass, but to-day I stopped where the paths cross and I walked down to the stream near Broomy with him, and he helped me across the bog. He told me of Europe and his wanderings there, and finally spoke freely. He has found in himself a healing power and his touch can relieve pain, and he knows this springs from the depths of his spirit and is God-given. If he were a woman he would be suspect as a witch but, as a man, he is free to roam the world and use his power as and when he will. He seemed to sense my sympathy and understanding, for I was also very aware of his sincerity and awe. We walked back towards Moyles Court together and finally I told him of my wrist which I twisted badly in January and is till stiff and painful. We sat in the sunshine by Dockens Water, and he has restored it. He was very still and silent as his hands moved close and a great warmth was round my wrist—a healing warmth—and then I knew the pain had gone. He left me there to go back to Gorley and I, alone, to Moyles Court, marvelling and free from pain.

Wednesday 3rd July

I awoke, and still—*no* pain in my wrist *at all*. I longed to meet my healer again (Richard, his name is) and, though I walked as far as Whitefield hoping to find him, the moors were bare and the movements only of deer and ponies in the glades and among the trees. Yesterday was only my third meeting with him, but I must find him again. I dare speak to no-one of my release from pain: there is so much fear and suspicion or open scepticism and scoffing that I would fear for his safety. Our blessed Lord healed like this and the resultant jealousy and suspicion led Him to His death. Richard is a *true* 'priest'—*true* 'guardian of the Sacred Fire'; how can he guard this flame, feed it, use it to warm, heal and restore us all without himself being destroyed? He told me he does not know how best to use his gift—whether to travel again, to get a job near here or to settle in some spot and be, there, a healer of body and spirit, alone. He *will* be guided aright, but—I know my people's attitude to him will be of fear and suspicion. What would the new apothecary in Ringwood say? With his scientific knowledge of the healing power of herbs and potions? What will John Hicks say about it? Will he accept this *spiritual* power? Or will our fears hold us back?

Thursday 4th July

Robert and Margaret over from Fordingbridge, and I asked Robert if he knew of Richard and of his home at Gorley. He has heard about them and says Richard's father is dying and unlikely to live much longer. There are two younger boys at home, and other sisters now grown up and away. I told him about my wrist, and Robert had heard of genuine powers like this, but I could feel he was cautious and reluctant to accept it and wanting to say I was gullible and swayed by Richard's charm. How slow and reluctant we are to accept miracles to-day, though we accept them in the gospels. I will accept *no* truth from the gospel that is not relevant, applicable and able to be demonstrated as surely to-day as then. Now that copies of, or parts of, the gospels are under every chambermaid's pillow and by every weaver's loom, we can form our own judgments instead of always being dependent on the scholar and translator. This is such an age of exploration, experimentation, journeying and discovering—as never before. My exploration is in the mind and heart of me—my journeying and discovering are in the magic and mystery of *people*, and the so-called "foolish" most of all, for they are less blinded by their own learning.

A letter from John Hicks. He is staying in Ringwood tomorrow night with Mr. Crofts and will be here on Saturday morning, take Sunday meetings and leave for Devon on Monday. He is always on the move, *dear* man.

Friday 5th July

After I wrote my diary yesterday I read this in a pamphlet brought by Margaret: "Retire into yourself and enter into your own faculties; you will find there God, virtue and the other universal and eternal truths." This seems to me the only answer to the new scientific search for truth. *All* the new revelations must be laid alongside our own intuitions and not until they are illuminated from within us shall we see their eternal truth—not merely mathematical measurements and catalogues, but the deeper truth as well, that poets and saints grope for. We must adore and not only examine. 'The Sovereign Judge will not call us to account for what we have done on someone else's authority: each will answer for himself.' I am a little surprised that Robert sent me this! He knows well that I cannot accept that the priesthood cannot err! There is a sense in which our country is freer to speak openly than ever before, and yet it must also speak in fear. Robert clings to his authority though a non-conformer. He dare not lead without it.

Saturday 6th July

Young James Dunne came in from Ringwood as it was getting dark, in great distress—tearful and exhausted, having run all the way through the fields. There had been a fair passing through to Dorset with cock-fighting and dog-fighting and bull-baiting and barbarous cruelties. An Irish wolf-dog, a tall stately creature, was beaten by a cruel mastiff, and a dog young James had known as a pup was thrown to the bull which tossed and gored and killed it, and killed two other dogs as well; and young James was sickened by such dirty pastimes and ran out to us in near hysteria. Thank God John Hicks was here and able to calm the boy. We let him stay for the night by the kitchen fire with the men who were here also for the haymaking. It was not a cold night but the boy was shivering and wretched. He has been apprenticed to a baker in Ringwood since May and is unhappy and goes back to his home in Warminster at the end of the year. He's a good lad and a faithful member of our meeting, but was always a bit simple and over-sensitive and restless. John H. came to look at the progress of the New Wing. He seemed reserved—"just bricks and mortar", he said—and I knew he wondered what life and thought would fill it, what purpose it would meet.

Sunday 7th July

John Hicks led our meeting. Few came to-day as many were held up by the hay which is partly cut and partly lying, and there were two heavy storms yesterday and it must be tossed. John spoke of miracles of healing and I marvelled for he said, "Too easily are our eyes closed and our ears stopped to the miracles around us, so that because of our unbelief we are unhealed". I told John later about the healing of my wrist, and he said he had known of people with this gift, not just the supersitition of the King's healings, but a truth behind witchcraft and magic and healing salves. He spoke of the Catholics' beliefs in the healing power of Christ through relics of the saints and crucifixes and the like. "I believe there is a truth hidden in both magic and witchcraft though I fear them both", he said. In Richard's healing I have no fear. John stayed in the granary all night. There is much Popish money-making in the selling of relics, and much trickery and deceit.

Why do we always try to get power for *ourselves* through these mysteries instead of being in awe, and learning? The new scientists and mathematicians have more humility in their discovering than most of us, unlearned ones, have in our searchings.

Monday 8th July

He (John H.) left early this morning—for Plymouth, he told me, to see a ship that was leaving for the New World. He was, he said, seriously thinking of joining the crew for he finds it almost impossible to hold to his faith when Catholics persecute his people and his preaching is suspect. He dare preach only the accepted Protestant position and his own private visions and insights are given only to a few—of whom I am one. He said he got strength from our support at Moyles Court, and I thanked God for that. 'A great prince in prison lies', John Donne has written. He who so strangely uses physical symbols to reveal spiritual truths may never have meant what I see in these words. The incarnate God was, and still is, imprisoned by humanity and by the prison of the flesh—but in Jesus he broke free. I see Mr. Hicks also struggling to break from his prison of church and priesthood to find the freedom of spirit and thought which is his true self. I believe if he goes to the New World he will renounce his priesthood and go a free man. Dare he? He has left me a copy of the book he wrote three years ago—"A Story of Illegal Suffering of Many Christians in Devon"—which sent him to London the following year on his petition to the King for restitution of fines. He is *right*, but he is outspoken and therefore in danger.

Tuesday 9th July

John is fighting two wars. One is in himself. He knows the truth and reality of his spiritual search. He knows the real journey of his life is to follow the leading of his spirit through fantasy and dream, insight and vision, to a higher plane. Yet he is timid and fearful, and his faith in the truth of vision fails so often. His other war is on life's surface where our Christian faith tries to express itself in robe and role, in church and chapel, in doctrine and dogma, and breaks in friction and feud, in extremes and extravagance, in hatred and hostility.

How can he fight these two wars at once without being broken in spirit or exiled in the flesh? I remember his face, full of pain, when he said, "Because of our unbelief we are unhealed". And I remember the quiet warmth and healing in my wrist. I twist and turn it, and all is *well*. And I remembered—"Each will answer for himself"—and I know, for me, the inner life of my spirit is all that I have and all that will go with me when I pass over. I dreamed last night that I was crossing Fritham bog, picking my way from one hummock to the next, and bog asphodel and cotton grass waved around my feet and the myrtle smelt sweet—and yet I was afraid.

Wednesday 10th July

We have had two days of heavy rain and the hay they tossed on Monday is sodden and only days of hut son can save it, and skies still overcast. I fear we shall lose a great deal. The building is now getting held up by the wet weather. Fortunately much of the building material has been moved from the coach-house and Ken has been able to put the little carriage and the coach back under cover.

The dream of Monday night, of Fritham bog and my fear, is still with me. Our dream world has more reality than we allow. I think dreams are as true as the truths of the Bible—metaphorical, and needing our own individual interpretation and insight for understanding. From hummock to hummock I went, in a world of sensual beauty, yet I was unsure of my direction and very near to bog and destruction, and it was fear that overwhelmed me. Life on the surface was good, but the earth had power over me, and the heavens were far away. I think there is a psalm about this?—Didn't he dream of drowning, and waves and storms submerging him?

Thursday 11th July

Rain all this week. They are very worried about the hay harvest. If we get no sun before the week-end it will be lost. We have had no summer yet—except for the roses, which are lovely, though dripping and heavy-headed. I have a bowl full in the front hall by the staircase—new buds.

News of the death of William, 5th (?) Earl Pembroke, bachelor, ne'er-do-well. Where next for Anne, I wonder? She managed the domestic side of Wilton House so well, and may now have to leave.

Friday 12th July

The outside building is held up by the rain, but I went to the carpenters' workshop (still in the coach-house) and watched them carving the panelling. The master-carver is such a nice person, pupil of Grinling Gibbons* and has become very friendly with Ken. He has brought two young apprentices with him—all of them from Salisbury and their work is good and quick. He hopes to finish his work by the end of the month and move on to Wimborne to restore some timbers in the Minster—commissioned by Mr. Ettrick the magistrate. Because of his skill he is never short of work, but seems to have no settled home. I then went to see the stonemasons who have built a cover for their work and a shelter so that are not hindered by the weather. It was noisy and dusty so I did not stay long, but they were carving heads for the ends of the beams—one I felt sure was meant to be Harriet! They were killing time, I think, as their work was ready for assembling, being just now mostly the window mullions.

Saturday 13th July

A wretched day for at first light a stranger came on horseback with a note for me. It was John Hicks' writing and I was over-joyed, expecting it to tell me he was coming back. It said, "I leave Plymouth to-day for the new World, on board a sturdy boat that I found, by chance, loaded and ready to leave at first light. We are a motley crew and the Captain only agreed to take me as I was ready to work as a galley hand, being, as you know, more landsman than sailor. Give my greetings to the Moyles Court group, for I love them dearly and cannot expect to see them again for many months. Indeed, how can I know I will ever return, for ahead of me all is unknown? I have told you often of my fears, and you will know why I must leave our troubled land. I must stand by the truth in my heart and not allow myself to be bound by acts of uniformity dictated by politicians and those who look for material success and acclaim. I shall soon be forgotten but you, I know, will not forget. I shall be strengthened when I remember your faith in

100

me, and you will always be in my thoughts and prayers. God bless you all. JH Keep what I have left in the granary safely for me."

Sunday 14th July

I went to Ellingham to church after a night of tears and loneliness. He has gone and I find it *so* hard to bear. I knew I had to come to terms with this and accept it by morning, for I would have to tell the group by evening. I thought the day would never pass, and it was a squally day of summer sun and heavy showers, and roses in the garden were ablaze. I thought of the ocean, and surely it must be squally to-day as he moved further and further away. I have no recollection of the service at Ellingham, except the prayer for peace—"whose service is perfect freedom"—and I thought, "*This* is why he has gone—to serve in freedom". But—what of his poor? In the evening the group met in the stable chapel, and I broke the news to them that Mr. Hicks had left for the New World. They were stunned. Anne Bolwell said, "Don't grieve, Mistress Lisle, many leave and many return, and not many seem to be gone for ever. I think he will return." She meant it kindly, but I must not want him back if his service to his Lord "in perfect freedom" cannot be given here. We prayed for him at the meeting and for his safety. No chance to-day to collect his things from the granary. What has he left there? First Bridget, now John.

Monday 15th July

I went up into the granary as dusk fell. No-one was about and I went round by the back, as the men (and the girls) were celebrating the end of a disastrous hay harvest at Rockford and I knew they would dance and drink too much and not look for me. I let Harriet go with the children to join them. I found the corner among the old husks and a broken sack of corn where John had slept, and in an old green cape found the things he had left and asked me to guard. There were quills and an ink-horn, and a small dagger and a carved drinking horn, and a small pewter pot with a wick in wax inside, and a collection of papers in his writing. I took them under the cape back to the house and found some of the papers to be material for another book, headed "A Discourse on the Excellency of the heavenly Substance". Such a heading was beyond my understanding! When he left a week ago had he *really* meant to sail for the New World so soon? Surely he would have taken this manuscript with him? I think often of his silly little wife, Abigail, who never really left her mother to be John's wife. But then he was too often away to be a good husband, too. She will stay in Portsmouth with her mother now, I suppose.

Tuesday 16th July

Rain fell again to-day and, although I knew there was the Rockford party last night, I had not fully realised what a disastrous harvest it has been. My heart has been heavy with other things. I am trying not to think John is running away—but—to the New World? Was he really feeling as bad as that? It seems so sudden a decision. I had got used to his going to Holland and France, and know that his friends there understood him. Some months back he had said something to me about having faith in the young James, Duke of Monmouth, as being the strong Protestant successor to the King. He is a popular young man, but so much gossip surrounds the King and the Duke's mother.

Sorted carefully again John H's belongings, and folded most into the green cape and stored them in my private chest—secure even from Harriet! The manuscript of the book I have stored away, but other papers I have laid aside to read first.

Wednesday 17th July

Found among John's papers a tattered piece covered in small writing (John's) and dated 1649, and a copy of something written by the Mr. Gerrard Winstanley of whom he spoke at his outpouring to me last June. For twenty-five years he must have kept this fragment close to him. I will copy it on the last pages of this journal and let the words speak to me as they have done and do (?) to him.* *Why* has he left these things behind? Will I ever know and understand this man? And yet, I do; in love and at depth, I do. What does knowing of details, of when, why and wherefore, matter when it is the whole man I love, the Christ in him wholly, not the parts?

Thursday 18th July

Nearly all the hay is lost; "Good for little but bedding", they say. This is grievous, and we can only pray and work for the corn harvest and hope this wet first half of July may bring in a later summer.* The only weeks with any feel of summer near were my weeks away—Chilton and London.

I realised to-day that a part of me has always been looking forward to John's next visit. Now that part is sterile and barren. No more forward looking. I must consolidate, relax, accept. Everything that was good in our relationship is good for ever and indestructable, for this is the nature of Love of the Christ.

When I put John's papers with his cape in my secret chest, I found a little chap-book I bought some years ago when I purchased ribbon and braid from a wandering pedlar. Turned over the pages idly, and found this for my comfort—

"—Absence dies, and dying proves
No absence can subsist with loves
That do partake of fair perfection".
(O.F.)

There is something close and special between John and me. I have never before known that Love that is ready to "lay down his life for his friend". Am I a silly old woman? No! Neither silly nor old, but wise and ageless?

Friday 19th July

In the thoughts and distractions of last week I never missed Phyllis, and this morning Jean came from the laundry to see me, to say that Phyllis ran away last Monday and returned last night, and—her pregnancy is over. "I have plans for the child," she had said, and I realised and did nothing. Now it is over, but Jean says she is very unwell and bleeding heavily. Went down at once to Ken's cottage to see her. Poor, silly girl! She had been to "Mother Black", the "Witch of Godshill", and been aborted. I don't know the old woman but everything suspicious gets put down to her. I tried to console her, and the whole family, and left her cleaned up and with, I hope, some wish to live, and begged Ken to keep away from her until she is stronger. She is a healthy girl and did not seem to me to want to die. I had taken herbs to heal, stop the bleeding and stimulate her, and told her to lie quietly until Monday when I would come again—unless they want me before. Told Ken to see me each morning with a report on her. When she is recovered she must live in the house here. Her presence there will ruin that family and that marriage; Phyllis is cruelly jealous of Ken's nice young Joanne and their children.

Saturday 20th July

Ken's cottage roof is leaking badly. It is not right for him to see the work on my new wing while his cottage falls into disrepair. I saw Pilbeam, and he has agreed to send a carpenter and thatcher up by the end of next week to repair it. This wet July has made matters worse and it must be done soon—even if patched up until drier weather. Ken says Phillis is "sleeping and sulky". I told him that when she is better I want her here to help me. "Thank you, Madam", he said, in a way that made me aware of what a problem she has been—and will be up here, no doubt.

Mr. Webb pressing me to finalise plans for the interior of the new wing.

Sunday 21st July

Peaceful, ordinary Sunday.

Bridget, if her voyage went well, could be home by now. Prayers for her safety, for Leonard's health and my granddaughter's happiness, and for John Hicks on his journey.

No special thoughts, and lovely and restful to have none. The hay is mostly lost, and Bridget has gone, and John has gone, and Phyllis's baby has gone, and my money has nearly gone, but—with all these things that could be a worry—I feel that all is *well*, ordered, controlled, directed—as it *should* be, as it is decreed by the Blessed Provider . . .

"Give me the pliant mind, whose gentle measure
Complies and suits with all estates;
Which can sit loose to a crown, and yet with pleasure
Take up within a cloisters' gates." (George Herbert)

And I saw a yellow wagtail by the stream and a lesser spotted woodpecker feeding her brood (a second one?) in a hole in the acacia tree.

Tuesday 23rd July

Old Harvard Hall:- As Bridget sketched it for me when we spoke of our plans. (They haven't built it, and if what Bridget fears befalls, they never will!)

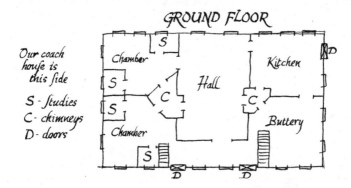

The second floor will have, above the Hall, a library, and the chambers at the back will have in each corner, studies for students, and the chambers in front, without studies, for tutors. I can adapt this with a meeting hall below and for dining, and a library above, with the gallery above where the new wing joins the old building.

Wednesday 24th July

Visited Lady Bankes at Kingston Lacy Hall as Mr. Webb told me they had just finished their new building and he would like me to see it before finalising the inside plans for the new wing. It is lovely, but on a much grander and more lavish scale than I can afford. She was welcoming, but I had to carry the weight of having been married to my husband and I felt I was suspect. She is a staunch Royalist—marvellous fighter over Corfe Castle in the Civil War. I spoke warmly *for* the monarchy, without difficulty! Ten years of widowhood and still I must live publicly in Sir John's shadow! "Till death us do part", but society does not see me as parted from him. Will women *ever* be allowed independent status? Most women widowed soon marry again, but I never will. I had too many weary years with myself trampled on, buried alive but never killed. Men can do what they like and I will never be killed, even if they take my head from my shoulders! I am of *no* party.

Thursday 25th July

Rain is easing off at last. Cloudy but with some bursts of sunshine, and the building is really looking good, with windows in place and roof timbers. The new building at Kingston Lacy is magnificent, but I am content, and will tell Mr. Webb my secret plans for the inside of the new wing.

Friday 26th July

A letter came to-day, a long one, from Bridget Dunch—after all these years! She and Edmund now live at Down Ampney House, near Cirencester, which she inherited from Uncle Antony Hungerford in 1659 (?). She has asked me to go and stay with them in August or September "before winter comes on". I am amazed, and pleased, and would love to go. Much will depend on how soon the building here is finished. "Surely old troubles can be buried with those who caused them?", she said. And I am hazy about those old troubles, but I think it was to do with my husband. Old Sir Antony left Bridget Lisle, John's mother, out of his will, although she was his daughter. It may have been political—Sir Antony was staunch Royalist and, of course, Sir John, his grandson, was *not*, and Sir Antony hated him for his support of Cromwell. But Edmund Dunch is Cromwell's cousin, and anyway those hot-headed, divided, confused days are far away now. I find it hard to work out who is who in that enormous, wealthy Hungerford family. They have land in so many parts of Wiltshire and Berkshire and Somerset and Gloucester, and when I was first married I was always meeting cousin this and cousin that. I loved my mother-in-law who was a child at Down Ampney, and I always liked Bridget Dunch, though we have not met for about thirty years!

Saturday 27th July

Spent some time trying to remember the Hungerford crowd. I always found the Lisles and Crokes difficult enough, after our much simpler White Beckonshaw line! It was easier in the Island where we met each other often, and everyone knew everyone. I want to accept Bridget's invitation so much. Perhaps early September? Started a reply to her to-day, telling her that I had a clear picture of Down Ampney left with me by my mother-in-law who was always telling my children of her childhood days there, tickling trout in the stream, her father's love of falconry, and keeping pet lambs, and weavers and spinners working in the cottages as well as in the mills. I wonder if it has altered much. We never visited there—because, I suppose, of John's unpopularity with his grandfather. I think his eldest sister was born there. I was thoroughly confused in August 1665, only a year after John's murder, when his brother William died only a month after stepson William's knighthood and the Island seemed full of their relations—many in the Island as the Plague raged in London and they had come down to escape it, mostly staunch Royalists, and I was suspect and glad to get back here.

Sunday 28th July

The rains this month have been the heaviest that anyone can remember in July. People blame popery and witchcraft, and say the weather shows God's anger with his people. That is why the Exchequer is bankrupt. That is why the Duke of York's son died. This is the judgment of God on the King's toleration of us, the dissenters!—or so say the Papists. Are they all *Jews*?—These adherents to Old Testament laws of vengeance and judgment? Are we not all, though in some very strange ways, struggling to be followers of Jesus Christ as in the New Testament? What about, "Blessed are you when you are persecuted for righteousness"? We seem all to be persecuted for that, and don't need a very wet July to make it plain! But there is still all this talk of "Sin" and "the fall of Adam"—and Church and State make capital out of this—even making laws to protect us from our sins! But yesterday the sun shone nearly all day, and to-day the clouds have *gone*! Is summer, at last, coming?

Monday 29th July

They have done Ken's cottage roof! I am very glad. Pilbeam seized the sunshine on Friday afternoon and sent two men and Ken and the thatcher from Harbridge, and they worked all through Saturday and left Ken to finish. Pilbeam inspected it this morning and said it was mainly the chimney end and will now be weatherproofed for many years. I am thankful, as I was afraid they would find more serious damage. Ken came to thank me and I told him that Phyllis should come into the house next Thursday. There is room for her with the other three girls next to Harriet.

The sun is making everything grow *so* fast since the earth's roots are well and truly watered. Enormous cabbage and spinach, and lovely beans and peas and all herbs, and onions and carrots growing so well. Though the hay was a disaster, if we get summer sun now there will be good oats and rye, and the fruit is well set.

Tuesday 30th July

Went with Harriet, Phyllis, Katie and Ken in the little carriage to Ringwood market. I should do this more often for I enjoy it so much. We went round the stalls and bought raspberries and cherries and early plums for bottling, and potatoes from France and shrimps from Christchurch, and smoked mackerel and some Dorset knobs and Cheddar cheese. I chose some damask for hangings and Harriet insisted that we needed more cords and braids and bindings— "Madam, I cannot use old ones again and again for ever!" She likes to feel she persuades me against my will, but I enjoy buying as much as she does. We bought two big slabs of gingerbread for them all to-night. Grannie Finch had her stall as always, selling candy and fudge and toffee apples, so I bought some for Phyllis and Katie to share with the children. I bought Ken a new horse brass and he showed me some lace he had bought for Joanne. Katie slipped in to see her mother near the White Hart, and Annie came out to greet us. We all enjoyed it and came back with baskets full, smelling of mackerel and shrimps and the dust of the market. We went in the morning and back by lunch, for by evening it is very rough and noisy, the best things sold and drink flowing.

Wednesday 31st July

I *did* enjoy yesterday's market—it reminded me of my childhood when I used to go more often. I enjoyed the greetings from friends, the caps doffed and the curtsies as we passed, and the crowds pushed back from the stalls as I moved towards them when we had left Ken and the carriage. But in the night I woke and felt ashamed, for I remembered John Hicks' words about the poor, about his serving them. I remembered my anxieties because of my inheritance, my responsibility for it and my unworthiness of it. Yet in Ringwood market I forgot it all and enjoyed my status and my friends of equal standing. I despised the smells and the stench of the poor, the rubbish they amass, and their poverty. Is this their destiny, as I know my own? Or is John Hicks right when he says we are *all* selfish and the poor have no-one to *fight* for them—the rich serve a few of them from their wealth, as I do? It seemed innocent enjoyment at the time but—in the night— I felt guilty. Now, in a new day—I'm confused! But look back and ponder on George Herbert's words I recorded just two Sundays ago.

AUGUST

Thursday 1st August

Phyllis came into the house to-day to live here, "for the time being", I said. Harriet is a wise person, and a loving one too. I thought she might be silent and critical of my decision, for much of the responsibility will be hers, as Phyllis is sharing the girls' attic next to Harriet and the sewing room. But she just said, "She has not had much chance to go straight, Madam—not with that mother. She is only brazen on top because of fear underneath. We'll help her, and she can learn to be proud of her father when she doesn't have to see him with her step-mother." A lot of shrewd commonsense there, and I pray she may be right.

Friday 2nd August

Finished my letter to Bridget Dunch after talking to Mr. Webb about the completion—yes, completion!—of the new wing. He says that it should be finished in the second half of September, so if I go to Down Ampney in the first week or so of September I will be back for the finish (and will miss the dreary days towards the end when I know I shall be impatient to have it finished). I said I was delighted to hear from her, and would pick up again, with great interest and pleasure, the news of her and her family, and that she must forgive the mistakes I shall make and my forgetfulness of the large Hungerford connections. Suggested I came between September 2nd and 14th—to suit her.

Saturday 3rd August

A letter to-day from Catherine. She and John got back from France two weeks ago and will stay in London until the 13th as they have an invitation to a military tattoo on the terrace at Windsor Castle on the 12th, enacting the story of the Dutch Wars. So they are back—after their four months' living well in

Court circles! I haven't seen John once this year! He and Typhena were so alike, and Bridget and Margaret were like each other. However hard we try to bring our children up, in the end they are themselves, unique and unpredictable! Is the whole of life really a stuggle to find a balance between freedom and obedience? "Whose service is perfect freedom". There is the answer, but it is not an easy solution, to find Him whom we would serve. Neither, having found Him, is the Way to serve Him in my own way; often I feel it is a half-hearted, feeble, too easy service. But—Moyles Court is my calling.

Sunday 4th August

Lovely to have a calm, quiet, untroubled Sunday. I do not even want to write here. "As God converse with God for evermore". Words only go so far. I would journey far beyond them, and, in meeting this morning, my soul went on a long journey—brought back by a butterfly on the window glass!

Monday 5th August

I suppose it is re-reading Catherine's letter and her mention of France and the Windsor Castle tattoo, and their way of life, so different from mine, that has made me think specially this morning of Tryphena. I suppose she is still in Wales. What a little tiger she was as a child! Very like her father, and son John was like him too, though opposite in politics. She was only a child (16) when she ran away to Lloyd, and I felt so guilty about it at first because I had been perhaps too harsh with her—trying to treat her as her father wished. She had always hung onto his every word. That is why, I suppose, she chose life with Lloyd. She is twenty-three now, and Bridget is in touch with her—and perhaps John is too. So she is not without family support. I would love to see her again, but most of all I would love her to want to see me—not because Bridget told her to, but because she wanted to. John won't encourage her. I can only hold my child in my heart and know her held in the heart of God, where there is understanding of her—as there is not in mine. (John's sister, Bridget, ran away when she was twenty, with the son of the local ironmonger; so to run away is not without precedent in the Lisle family!)*

Tuesday 6th August

Wrote to Catherine—a letter to greet them on their return from London. I have suggested a picnic at Linford Brook one day (any day) in the week following their return. I will ask Margaret and family too. The children would enjoy that, though Charles is seven years older than James (or six), but cousins should keep in touch with each other.

Saturday 10th August

Beautiful week of August heat and sunshine. I have sat in the shade in the garden each afternoon this week under the acacia, and read—but not much! Mostly I drowsed—and thought—and mused—and wondered. John H? Has he found his way? Not his way over the world's ocean, but his way across the ocean of his life—his soul's journey? I wonder. I wonder if I will ever know? Yet, our paths *will* cross and we will meet again. I *know*, with a strange certainly, quite unreasonable, but strangely sure, that our lives are inter-woven, even if this does not become clear until, at, or after, our death.

Why do I write a diary? I think I may give it up! My thoughts are of little value once they have surfaced and disappeared!

These hot, leisurely days (and nights) are for dreaming and drowsing—not for putting thoughts into words.

Sunday 11th August

Ellingham Church was cool and shady, and I was glad to be out of the heat for a little. Yes, I was glad to be there! That is a thought worth recording in this lazy week. I have not even been near the new building, but the distant sounds have made it clear that they are still working.

Monday 12th August

A kind letter from Bridget Dunch suggesting that, if I leave here on September 2nd, she will send their horses to Avebury on September 3rd. There is a good coaching inn and "you may be interested in the strange stones there", and her horses and coachman will bring me to Down Ampney on the 4th. "Stay as long as you wish", she says, "though I understand you will want to be back before very long, with your brave building enterprise so near completion". So, if I leave her on the 12th I should be home on the 14th. That all sounds good, and I feel very content about this whole visit. It feels a right and healing thing to do. I would be glad to be better known, and perhaps understood, by Sir John's side of the family. I think and hope that Dibden John will be gratified too. Strange that I should, twice in one year, journey northwards—once to Bulstrode and now to the Cotswolds. In fact, it has already been a full and busy year—with still a third to go.

Tuesday 13th August

The lovely proper summer weather continues. We needed sunshine so much after the dreadful weather in July, and indeed, too much cold and wet most of the year. Our rye and barley are looking good but not until it is safely under cover can we really take stock for the winter.

Seven weeks since Bridget sailed and nearly five since John H. left. It is hard to think of them in that other world; easier to think of Bridget, for she told me so much, but it is all hardships and difficulties. But—John?—I can visualise *nothing*. Somehow I cannot feel he is there—it seems so alien that I even wonder if his boat ever arrived. Perhaps he was drowned. Oh, God, hold him safe, for where Thou art, there is he also, as he is in my heart, where Thou art also. I folded rosemany and verbena into his cloak to keep the moth away.

Wednesday 14th August

Margaret has sent a note to Dibden to suggest the picnic for to-morrow—the only day when Robert is free. They will come from Fordingbridge anyway, to pick me up, and we will picnic at Linford and hope the Dibden family will join us. Sent a note to tell me and asking me to "do" the picnic! I am glad to! It must be the same fare they always had children—cold pigeon, and hard-boiled eggs, and lettuce and tomatoes, and little cottage loaves and gingerbread and toffee apples for the children, and the flagon of cider cooled in the brook. The peaches are ripe against the orchard wall, too, and perhaps Harris will find late raspberries. Katie helped Harriet and me to put it all ready to pack to-morrow in the big baskets.

113

Thursday 15th August

John and Catherine arrived from Dibden for the picnic. Margaret and the children had picked me up, with the baskets, as planned. I brought Katie—a mixture of work and pleasure for her! Robert, of course, had "other things to do" and never came! (He and John are not a good mixture!) John and Catherine and grandson Charles arrived at the bridge—only half-an-hour after us, and so we all met again for the first time since last Christmas! Charles has grown taller and has looks of my husband. Catherine pale and thin, but she never seemed very robust. John unchanged, and a little warmer towards me than he often is. It was a happy reunion. The children paddled and young Charles helped James climb the trees "looking down the river for the Dutch Navy", and Katie served out the food prettily and then took charge of Jenny and Sir John stamped around to beat the adders away and shouted to the children to wear their pattens every moment out of the water. When we had fed ourselves and the children and the chaffinches, and Katie had repacked the baskets, we four sat in the shade and shared each other's news. What different lives we are all leading!—J. and C. have had a very good time in France (Charles speaks French easily now). I had much to tell about the visit to Chilton Foliat,* about Bridget, and the new building, and about going to Down Ampney. We called the children so that Charles could tell us all about the Dutch wars as seen from Windsor terrace!—And so we parted again. A day of sun and a good reunion.

Friday 16th August

—And in the night massive thunderstorms and lightning. We just got our picnic in in time, for I heard the rain pouring down in the early hours, and the heat wave is ended. Was afraid the crops might have suffered badly, but they say it will depend on the next few days. The children were exchanging riddles at the picnic yesterday, and Charles produced this one from France which delighted James:-

"Two legs sat down upon three legs and had one leg in her hand, then in came four legs and bore away one leg, then up starts two legs and threw three legs at four legs and brought back one leg."

One leg — leg of mutton
two legs — woman
three legs — stool
four legs — a dog.

Saturday 17th August

Sunshine back again between showers; cooler and a blue sky full of billowy clouds. I have had two lazy weeks, with only the picnic interrupting quiet, orderly days. I said I would drive over to Dibden on Thursday for the night. Catherine is trying so hard to make peace between John and me, and I also want peace between us and feel our discordance is only because John thinks my political and religious views are all because of his father's influence over me. That is my fault, I suppose, and I should feel proud of my success if I indeed persuaded John that I was really in sympathy with his father. If only he could realise that I belong to *no* party—neither in politics nor religion. How much easier it would be if I could be content to be labelled—a This or a That or Another—then everyone could decide if they were for or against me. Then they could call me traitor or true! But I live to find God and good in every man—failing often, I know, but not yet so exhausted that I give up the struggle and, though other people feel safer hidden behind a label (John H. and the priesthood), *I* will not play for such simple safety.

Sunday 18th August

The corn is in! Rye, oats and barley. They have saved what they could, but it has not been an easy harvest and we shall be very short this winter.

Monday 19th August

I went out to look at the fields to see how the crops had survived the Friday storm. I had not realised they had already cut and carted one of the fields by the Ringwood path, and the other side of the path is stooked. The rest seems a little flattened in some places, but I called Farmer Mitchell and he came round with me and said it seemed to him that if the weather holds this week we would get some more in. I said, "I'm sorry we lost so much of the hay", and he said, "One

115

thing a farmer learns, my lady, is the meaning of give and take. The Lord gives and the Lord takes away. He keeps us on our toes and when He seems to let us down He balances it out in His own good time." I find wisdom in these country people that I never found in London!

Tuesday 20th August

The rain held off to-day, though there are heavy thunder showers about and Ringwood had a downpour. If we get a dry night they will cart some more to-morrow. I hope not to have to buy grain for the winter, for prices are soaring and the weather has been bad all the year and harvests poor throughout the country, and last year was not good either.

Wednesday 21st August

Rather a nasty accident to-day. Tommy Fowler from Poulner was riding on the hay-wain and was trying to shoot rooks with his catapult, and fell off, and the wheels of the cart behind went over him before they could pull up the horses. He should not have been on the wain, but no-one would accept responsibility for that. He broke his collar-bone and leg—the first probably in the fall, and then the leg under the wheel. Poor lad! They brought him here on the drop-end of the wain and sent for me. We splinted his leg and bound his arm to his chest with a sling, and he was very shocked and kept calling, "It's my brother's catapult and I've lost it". James Dunne found it and brought it to him, and Tommy managed a wan smile and James, of course, beamed with pleasure. I sent at once for Mr. Bolwell who came out with a friend who is a surgeon and bone-setter, and by evening Tommy was easier and in less pain. His father and brother came to take him home, but I said it was better not to move him or jolt him until to-morrow, and Mr. Bolwell and the surgeon would come and visit him in his home to-morrow evening. I am glad, if it had to happen, that it was to-day and not to-morrow, as I'm hoping to go to Dibden in the morning.

Thursday 22nd August

They carried Tommy home on a wattle hurdle. He seemed reasonably comfortable and Mr. Bolwell will see he is

116

properly tended. I reached Dibden soon after 2 o'clock—and glad to arrive for it was raining all day and the forest was very heavy with rain and summer growth. There are great areas of open moorland now where the trees have been felled for the King, and no sign of any replacement. The heather is in full flower and smelling of honey, but it can hardly be called "Forest" round Burley and Denny Lodge. The Dibden scene is much as before, and they seem to have settled into the home routine again. That house always depresses me; it is very full of old Croke possessions—furniture and portraits and old silver—all old-fashioned things that they never seem to want to change. But then they are away a lot and John has his boat and sails over to the Island or up the Beaulieu River, or to Lymington, so probably does not notice, and of course to Catherine they are home. We had a pleasant meal and were kept indoors by the weather. Charles had to recite to me in French, which he did not enjoy, and I was duly appreciative, and Catherine prattled away about France and worked at her new French tapestry.

Friday 23rd August

I have done my duty, and so have they. We were all very polite to each other and were careful to keep off all controversial subjects. But I think they heave a sigh of relief when I have gone—as I do. John came with me as far as Beaulieu (a little out of my way) for he had lent one of his boats to one of the Montagus and he will sail it back home from Bucklers Hard. He was able to be very grateful to me for the lift, so that was good. He had been over to Wootton to see William* who is still very crippled by his broken thigh—six months after the hunting accident. It seems that the bones are not properly knit and he is likely always to be lame. I am very sorry. He is a good man. I wish they lived on the mainland; I see very little of them.

So, home again.

Saturday 24th August

A peaceful day. More anxiety about the crops for there are still storms about and bursts of summer sun never last for long. My mind has been on family this week and I have given little thought to the building. The weather has not held them up, which is marvellous, and each week shows great advances. My mood about it swings from anxiety to delight, from fear of being caught in the development boom of the last years to certainty that it is the right thing to do. Too late to change my mind, and I must make it the best possible thing—to meet genuine need.

Sunday 25th August

Both in our meeting and at Ellingham we had the thought of "Some Paul and some Apollo, some Cephas, some Christ" and "All one body". Our divisions are both right and wrong; right for we *must* be faithful to the Christ within; wrong because we are all one in Christ (they are trying to persuade Presbyterians to remain within the Anglican church, but—bishops, though without the political power they had before the Restoration, are still the Anglican authority, and the Presybterians will stand out against that). For once, I was glad to be both in and out of the Church.

Monday 26th August

Little old Patsy Flannigan turned up. I haven't seen her since last autumn, but there she was as usual, down by the ford, sitting against the post with her huge bundle beside her, muttering as always. "Hallo, old Patsy", I called, and she rooted in the old bundle, still smelling of fish, and brought out her usual fairings and spread them on the ground. She looked up and saw no gleam of interest in my eye, so back to root in the bundle, deep down this time, grunting, pulling things out, discarding them. Then she pulled out a little package, wrapped in a grubby rag, looked up at me then back to the rag, and began to unfold, unfold, unfold. Finally, a wrapping of softer, cleaner stuff, and then—a little leather-bound, gold-clasped chap-book. A beautiful little thing. "To Anthea—Robert Herrick—died this year of grace 1674", it said on opening, and it is a charming little love poem. I always buy something from old Patsy and this was an unusual little treasure. I gave her a pound, and she chuckled and muttered and we both parted happily. 'Off to drink your money, Madam', said Harriet; and I—to drink my love poem.

Tuesday 27th August

It is a lovely little chap-book I got from old Patsy yesterday. Who was this Anthea?—and Robert Herrick who died this year?—I, old enough to know better, old enough to have grown out of loving, know and am still learning of love, and learn a little more of it through a treasure hidden in the depths of an old crone's bundle!—"bid me die, and I will dare E'en death, to die for thee".

Wednesday 28th August

Not surprising that John H. was much in my mind. Why do I feel so strongly that he is *not* in the New World? I feel him nearer than that. I awoke very suddenly, sat up, and had an "awake dream". He was at the foot of the bed, with his hat in his hand. "It is beginning to clear", he said, and, "You are right". Right?—in what way does he see me as right? What is coming clear for him? Is it my fear that he was running away from something in himself? Is it the *way* in which he must fullfil his destiny that is coming clear to him? He disappeared, and I heard myself saying Robert Herrick's words, "I'll dare, e'en death to die for thee".

Friday 30th August

I have let them all know that I am going away on Tuesday. There is always some excitement, I think, at the thought of being on their own. Pilbeam and Harriet between them can manage most things, but it is a comfort to me to know Mr. Webb will be in and out. The children all look at me in amazement—"Will you be away for long, Ma'am?", Hetty asked. "Not long", I answered, and thought, "How long is 'long' when you are only five?".

Saturday 31st August

Dear Katie! She is eyeing me sadly with those big hazel eyes! She had so hoped I would want her to come with me to Down Ampney! But this is too delicate and important a visit for me to take these young girls as a training experience for them. Harriet is very pleased that I have asked Caroline, her older sister, to come. She is a skilled needlewoman and very good with her hands in so many ways, and she will be a companion for me, since I got to know her well when she used to stand in for Harriet (her baby James's croup, and measles later, etc.). She came in to-day with pretty little herb pillows and cushions edged with lace for pins, and bunches of lavender twisted with coloured ribbons. "Shall we take them as gifts, my lady?— they are all from your garden!" A sweet and welcome idea.

To-day was *not* all sweet and welcome, but bustle and preparation, and Harriet fussed because leather straps for my chest were lost ("Who this time?"). They turned up later. I feel so calm about this visit, and the deeper anxiety because I want it to go well is over-ruled because of my great certainty that it is *right* to go. A rightness that creates a calm at the heart of me, stilling surface anxiety.

SEPTEMBER

Sunday 1st September

Final walk around and in and out of the new wing. Wood carvers (Grinling Gibbons' ex-student and his apprentices) at work on pieces for mantel and balustrades—"Harriet" (stone corbel!) grinning above the window, and other stone faces too. New plaster drying on the canvas. It *is* getting on, though still a lot to do and clear away before it can be called finished. Yes! To get away for some days will stop my anxious impatience! I commended each brick and stone and pillar and carving to my God—it is done for His glory, from the heart of me, and for love of his people, and may all that ever happens in that place be for good and for love of Him. "A man that looks on glass . . . may, if he pleases, through it pass . . . and heaven espy".

Packing, packing, packing—marvellous to be able to leave it to Harriet and Caroline, and know they are far more efficient about it than I would ever be. Shall take my diary this time!

Monday 2nd September

Left after noon for Wilton. It was an unhurried departure which was good, and I was glad I had decided to spend to-night with Anne. She is still in her wing of the house and will stay there until next spring and then see how the Seventh Earl plans for the running of the house and estate. William was so unwell all this year, and I think there must have been relief all round when he died in July, for the management was sadly neglected and Anne could do little about it. But she was her cheerful, happy self! Still looking immaculate and in the height of fashion! And she never seems to mind when I use her as a hostelry!

121

Tuesday 3rd September

Left fairly early and am now safely in Avebury and writing in this very comfortable coaching inn. The Dunchs seem well known here and the best room has been reserved for me. I have been well fed with pigeon and herb pie and their own damson wine and rye bread and a special local cheese. We had a good journey, by the Avon most of the way, through little villages with pretty little colourful cottage gardens and farms well-kept. After I had rested a little (we arrived about 3 o'clock and found the Dunch coachman and horses already here), a pretty little serving girl came up to say that, if I wished, her master would take me to see the strange old stones of Avebury. It was a cool, breezy day—grey and over-cast when we left Wilton but clearing skies as we came north. I said I would be very interested, called Caroline to accompany me, and we had a fascinating hour in the evening cool, (one of Dunch's men and Ken followed behind us—I appreciated their attentive guarding of me!). In many ways these Avebury stones are more impressive, though less massive, than Stonehenge. There are so many of them (two circles and an outer ring) and they cover a vast area. We climbed down a ditch and up on to a higher mound, and saw them clearly—many are very close to the village! Druids? Ancient British Kings' coronation grounds? No-one seems to know.

Wednesday 4th September

My men and horses set off early for home, and we only one hour later. Lovely run from Avebury, ending up on an ancient, straight, grassy track high up, and we passed into a new world of soft, grey stone—even stone-slated roofs to the cottages whose gardens were protected from sheep by stone walls, and sheep, sheep, everywhere!—and little, barefooted children running about and waving. And then—Down Ampney House—through the great, grey stone gates, clipped yews, box-hedges (like mine), huge chestnuts and limes and cedars—and I had arrived.

Oh, they are being good to me and kind, and Bridget—rather older than me, I think—said, as she kissed me good-night and left me with Caroline in their guest chamber looking

122

towards the church and the vast sky—"Alice, for some reasons, I have always felt a great sympathy with you, and wished we met more often. Your husband and mine had much in common, and were both loyal to Lord Cromwell, though my Edmund was quieter and less fiery than your John—but it is hard for women, for we must always show loyalty first to our husbands and suppress our own ideals and visions. They oppress us, and we are not free. Perhaps you and I will be able to talk freely together while you are here." I wept when she had gone—on Caroline's shoulder—for I had not realised what a deep, lonely ache had built up inside me and she had touched my pain—a kind, caring, healing touch.

Thursday 5th September

Awoke very early to sounds of horses on the gravel and men's voices calling, and looked out on the enormous Cotswold sky—what a long time ago that seems as the day ends and I write this by candle-light before finally to bed. It has been a day full of variety and interest. Edmund has two of his friends staying here, and his son Hungerford, and they were out early with falcons and dogs, and came back at about noon. Bridget took me over to the church in the morning, where there is a magnificent memorial to John's grandfather and his uncle in the Hungerford Chapel, and tablets to Bridget's sister and another of John's uncles—and others. We walked round the garden and then through the fields to a little stream, and it is—the Thames! (It is called the Ampney Brook but runs into the Thames only a short way away, near Cricklade.)—Yes, the same Thames of Westminster and Greenwich! I stooped and let little drops run through my fingers and slip back and bustle away to London, to carry the ships and barges to the world's oceans. Those tiny drops! Bridget and I were happy together and I loved the really warm companionship she gave me—and tried to give it in return.

They gave a welcoming dinner for me (a *banquet*!) in the evening—at least twenty guests, all rather rich and prosperous (Wool!); some neighbours and some family, and all inviting me to visit them, and I heard Bridget arranging things, "To-morrow morning?", "On Saturday?". I'm being cosseted and honoured, and I'm loving it!

123

Friday 6th September

Cirencester market in the morning—a sheep market!—
Pedlars and tinkers as well, of course, and barrows of vegetables and apples and pears and cheeses, but mostly bleatings
and shoutings of sheep and men and the smell of wool and
great sacks of fleece. We drove round in Bridget's little
carriage and stopped to look at great rolls of woven woollen
cloth, and then to a tavern on the edge of the town to wait for
Edmund and his drovers and shepherds to finish their business (they came in to market earlier than we did). Edmund
and his friends joined us and we had cider and local cheese
and fresh rye bread and pickles, and plums picked off the tree
for us by the landlord's young son. Hungerford took
Edmund's friends off to see Cricklade—he was M.P. there in
1659—and Edmund came in the carriage with us, he driving.
'I'll take you through the villages', he said, and we went to
three Ampneys—Crucis, St. Mary, St. Peter—and then to the
tiny hamlet of Harnhill—and found in the little Saxon
churches strange carvings: Michael and the dragon, lions and
serpents and strange symbolic figures. "They knew the battle
of good and evil as much as we do", Bridget wisely said. Back
to a quiet evening and one of the first fires of winter in the
parlour (it was a dry but blustery day and the evening chill).
The great hall of this house is very splendid—where we had
dinner last night—but too large to be cosy in the evening.
Moyles Court seems of another world! Harriet! My children!
John H.! New building!

Saturday 7th September

A misty morning and fine drizzle. First rain since leaving
home. Early autumn cobwebs on the lawn. Bridget wants to
take me over to the Sackvilles at Bibury Court on Monday,
and they have suggested we stay the night. "I don't want to
crowd too much into your visit", Bridget said, "And I don't
want to rush you". We discussed it and agreed to stay for the
night, so to-day has been leisurely and we have had time to
talk about the deeper things. Bridget has come to terms with
Anglicanism and uses the new Book of Common Prayer faithfully—"I know it by heart and treasure all its phrases and
teachings", she said. I wish I did. Some of us seem born to
learn through conformity, and others need the stimulus of

revolt. Jesus said, "I am the Door", and we must use it to go both ways—in *and* out. And we talked of the new growth of alchemy, leading to explorations undreamed of in mathematics and chemistry. And we spoke of the new machine age into which we are moving—sthat, after visiting spinners and weavers at work in the cottages. The mist cleared and clouds lifted and though it was overcast we walked over the fields to Latton, by the little Ampney Brook, and had griddle cakes and damson wine with the farmer's wife there. Cotswold barns are huge—much bigger than the cottages—all built of this yellow-grey stone—for storing wool as well as corn. A cosy fire again and soon to bed.

Sunday 8th September

Strange—and friendly and good—to have the church almost in the garden and to watch the congregation arriving before we have even left—and then walk across just as the bell stopped ringing! And strange, for me, too, to be a nobody there. All my feelings of hypocrisy at being there fell away, for I set an example to no-one and was there out of love and respect for God in my friends and God in me and God in that place where we gathered together. So I was receptive and open to receive; so I did receive. I found the service holy, reverent and real. The vicar mumbled hastily and I couldn't hear. Yet—it *was* holy, reverent and real. Was it because Bridget was by my side and I "caught" her feeling for it all? Never mind why. I was able to pray in prayer-book words and felt at one with them all.

Drizzled in the afternoon and we sat in the library and B. told me that her mother and uncle were friends of Dr. John Donne and she showed me a book of his poems sent to "Mistress Dunch", after the Dean's deaths, by his son. I shared with her my memory of George Herbert, and we agreed that ours was an age of reaching out in every direction, over the oceans, by microscope and telescope, by science and philosophy, but deepest, richest, furthest, the spiritual outreach, not just in Bible study but the searchings in solitude expressed by the Herberts and Donnes and Miltons of our age, and through all the "devices which help us to glimpse the invisible", (Bridget).

125

Monday 9th September

Edmund's friends and Hungerford left in the morning, and Edmund decided to come with us to Bibury. He wasn't well last winter—gets bronchitis badly—and Bridget is glad he is coming. "He stays out too long and catches cold", she said, "I'd rather he was with us". Oh, what a day it has been! We had a lovely drive on a nearly straight track over the grass-lands, straight across Akeman Street where we saw the actual old Roman stones still on the road, and so to Bibury Court. It is a splendid house, much of it modern, finished in 1633 by Sir John's father, Sir Thomas. (Bridget's uncle). We rested in their beautiful parlour and then had a huge meal, beautifully served—young lamb roast with herbs, and potatoes, roast as well (new to me done that way!)—And apple dumplings and cream! Then Sir John had to deliver some newsletters (about wool prices) to two near-by villages and asked us to go for the drive. It was *so* beautiful. There was a bigger and more splen-did tythe barn at Ablington than I had ever seen, and the river Coln, at Coln St. Aldwyn, wound through the meadows, clear and lovely. "Full of trout", John said. So, back again, and friends of the Sackvilles to dinner. (More beautiful food! Too much for me!). They all seemed rich and friendly and all with vast estates. (Sheep need a lot of open space so their owners need it too, I suppose.)

Tuesday 10th September

Edmund was out early with John, flying falcons. We all gathered for breakfast by about 10 o'clock, and Bridget and I walked to the village, past a new row of weavers' cottages, over the little bridges across the Coln, to the great mill where we watched the corn being ground, and then back over the meadows. More food!—pasties this time, and pies—and then we left for Down Ampney. There was something good about that journey home—not just the bracing air of that lovely grassy track, and it had been a lively and fascinating visit to Bibury—but Down Ampney House has a welcoming peace about it that wraps me round. "Well done, Alice!", Bridget said, "I didn't warn you that you would have to eat too much at the Sackville's". We had a peaceful supper round the par-lour fire—biscuits and cheese and plum cake and wine—and talked of books and poetry and our children and our anxieties about them, and small homely things that make up the world of wives and mothers. Then Edmund came in and finished the biscuits and the cheese, and we all had more wine and cake, and then to bed. Caroline has had a busy two days as well, I gather. "What a lot there is to learn", she said, "And you don't realise it until you get away from home". We slept soundly.

Wednesday 11th September

Early Autumn—sitting by Ampney Brook:

> Pink frayed fronded grasses hide the lark beneath my feet;
> The tall blades reach the sky and clouds behind the meadow-sweet.
> Deep crusted earth shows hoof-marks and slots of vanished deer
> On the sheep-worn track beside me, over the downland clear.
> Breezes the only movement and tearing grass the sound,
> As sheep with relentless motion wrench the grass-blades from the ground.
> Near to pure silence, near it, though the song of the infant Thames
> Gurgles and whispers and murmurs and bubbles with crystal gems.
> A bee burrows deep in the clover—then high in the sky above
> The lark from the choirs of heaven, like the first baptismal dove,
> Breaks through the clouds' sound barrier and pours on the listening ear
> The joy of each thing in creation, unique, beloved, most dear.

Thursday 12th September

So, to-morrow I leave this lovely place. What a happy visit it has been—gentle, soothing, altogether restful and healing. Bridget has been *so* good to me—nothing too much trouble— and she has drawn me into the household and made me feel at home in every way, and I have loved them all.

I found a book here of a play by John Fletcher—old now,

127

but this extract, when I read it, breathed Down Ampney to me:-

We are arrived among the blessed islands
"Where every wind that rises blows perfumes . . .
The treasure of the sun dwells here, each tree . . .
Serves to bring forth immortal fruit.
The very rivers . . :
Throw up their pearls, and curl their heads to court us
. . . Nothing that bears a life, but brings a treasure."

I am loaded with gifts!—The lovely woollen shawl from Bibury; a pure white fleece from Edmund and Bridget to go on my bed at home; a huge Gloucester cheese and a flagon of local cider and a great leg of mutton to celebrate my home-coming, dressed with bunches of herbs—mint and rosemary and thyme and marjoram. The little gifts I gave seemed so small, but Bridget says that Caroline has worked marvels during the week, mending her linen and laces and repairing the hall brocades "which will now last us many winters".

Friday 13th September

Managing the homeward journey with only one night's stay. The waggon was mostly packed last night and we left early, reaching Avebury to change horses soon after noon. We made Amesbury by dusk and stayed at the Abbey guest house, so to-morrow we shall easily get home.

Saying good-bye at Down Ampney was *so* hard! As we turned out of the drive gates I remembered how apprehensive I had been only just over a week ago when I arrived! How different now—feeling I really "belong" to part of John's family, as never before. We turned left and crossed the bridge over my Ampney Brook and I saw the spire through the trees and the roof of the house and a glimpse of my bedroom window—and then they were gone. Caroline has enjoyed it very much as well. She has learnt to spin and card wool and watched woolpack races and Cotswold Morris men on Latton green, and is taking corn dollies back as gifts. So—our journey home is going well. Ken, at Avebury, as good as ever and on time. "You will be pleased with your building, I think, Madam". And so I look forward again to Moyles Court and my house-hold—richer and more blessed than when I went away.

Saturday 14th September

What a noisy hostelry! Dogs barking and much shouting—men and women—outside and below my window. And they seemed to be arriving and leaving all night long. I slept little, but had so much to think about, threads to lay down and threads to pick up, that it would have been a night of little sleep anyway. We left speedily in the morning and soon were passing Old Sarum, and there was Salisbury's giant spire ahead (I thought of my little slim Cotswold one), and then all familiar landmarks, Downton, Breamore, Hyde, Gorley, Mockbeggar, and through my gates and Moyles Court again. What a welcome! I was home! And happy to be home!

Very soon I was escorted to see the building. Everyone from the house followed—even Henry and Philip and the men from the yard! (I think they have all had a good look round while I have been away.) *So* much has been completed, all the panelling in place and plastering done, and Mr. Webb told Pilbeam that the craftsmen and all hired labourers will be paid off and leave next week, and then we shall see to the final clearance, make good the drive, etc., and the work will be complete! Oh, God, I am thankful, grateful, amazed. "The heaven of heavens cannot contain Thee, how much less this house which I have built".

So now to bed, tired, proud, feeling somehow my father's blessing—and perhaps even Sir John's?

Sunday 15th September

Awoke to the strangest sounds under my window! A squeaky whistle, repeated and then on another note, and then a few more, and another odd whistle. Then, very hesitant and faltering, neither time nor rhythm, but recognisable—"Greensleeves"! When it was finished there were quiet steps on the gravel and then silence. Later, I asked Harriet about it. "Oh, Madam, that poor James Dunne! The ostler's boy from St. Giles was over and showed him how to make a reed pipe and we have had him struggling for days." I sent for him and gave him a wedge of Gloucester cheese and thanked him. He said, "They call me mad, my lady, but they don't know the world I live in, where the poor are rich for they dance and sing, and the rich are poor for they have no dreams, and the

poor are rich for they are naked and the rich are poor in pris-
ons of castle and palace".

A day of unpacking and sorting—apples for the children
and cider for the men—and of course the joy of our Sunday
meeting—I felt I had been away for months in a foreign
country! (Harriet pleased with her little woollen stole from
Ciren.) The Ringwood and Linwood folk all came and we
shared out honey cakes the Whittington family gave me at
Bibury, and I felt our world was enlarged and embraced all
the Cotswold families—Catholics, Anglicans, Protestants
and nonconformers—bound by "broken honey cakes and
cider"— a *real* sacrament!

I needed a day of rest! Spent the afternoon quietly sorting,
tidying, stilling my spirit. Both Bridget and John Hicks must
be safely in the New World by now (Could they meet? They
never have).

Monday 16th September

Old familiar sounds—tunes being sung, chippings, hammer-
ings and trundlings, and voices calling, the odd angry shout,
and I did my ordinary things in the ordinary way—and—
whenever I go away I come back apprehensively, expecting
troubles to clear up and sort out. So often it has been so, and
seemed always to be so when Sir John was alive, whether in
London or the Isle of Wight; but this year I have been lucky
and have been at home for the unexpected happenings.
Harris has a nasty poisoned hand and I am dressing and
poulticing it, and one of the apprentices ran a chisel into his
wrist the day after I went, but that is healing. A riderless horse
was caught at the ford and empounded but claimed by a
stranger (highwayman?) two days later. Small things they tell
me little by litle. Phyllis "behaved herself", Harriet said. All
is *well*.

Tuesday, 17th September

Autumn days of misty trees and turning leaves and wet weeds
in the borders and spiders' webs.

Mr. Webb over, and will come again on Thursday and
hopes completion day will be Friday, and would I keep the
day free for final inspection with him. Is that day really to

come at last? My visit to Down Ampney fitted in *so* smoothly—as all this year seems to have done.

Wednesday 18th September

Quiet, normal, silent day. No words to write. No thoughts for words. Time quickly works her miracles, whether we are aware or not. Miracles of healing and resurrection.

Thursday 19 September

Needed these "normal days" and now feel refreshed with a sense of accomplishment. Oh, John H, I miss you and you feel small and so far away—and I want you here—to feel you again. There is a security when you are with me, though I have never known anyone as insecure as you! I go over, in my morning prayers, all those I love. "Commend them to Almighty God", the priests would say, as if God might forget them! No—*He* reminds me of *them*, and gives me His power in that memory—for their service. They can say always, "I know she is behind me!" That thought may be strength to them—Love's strength.

Friday 20th September

They have finished! Mr. Webb came and asked me to go round with him in the afternoon for he said his work for me was completed on the site and only the final reckoning remained, which he would draw up when he knew I was satisfied. How could I be otherwise? I slipped in last night and gasped with delight. I tried to appear calm and critical and cool as we went round together. But I am very pleased, and very grateful to him. Now we must polish and furnish and dedicate, and then—use it! He knew I was pleased, and said he had been pleased too by the way everyone had worked together. When he had finished the inspection the men were all gathered outside and I praised them and publicly thanked Mr. Webb and Pilbeam and all the craftsmen—stonemasons and carpenters and bricklayers and labourers—and sent for the best barrel of ale and every tankard in the house, and we all drank to honest labour and skilled workmen, to builders and architects, and Mr. Webb called out, "Let us drink also to Mrs. Lisle who has been the one who had the vision and knew what she wanted and has made us see it through". So we were all inordinately proud and happy! And I shook them all by the hand and Mr. Webb gave me the keys and they all left.

Saturday 21st September

Set everyone to work in the new wing this morning! Oh, the polishing and waxing of floorboards and pannelling, and sweeping and mopping and dusting, and the men carried over what furniture I could spare (my locked chest with John's papers and cloak into "his" room), and two lovely old Elizabethan carved chairs from Grandfather Beconshaw which never looked right in the house and no-one ever sat in them. The good furniture from the loft which came down with me from the London house was brought over and cleaned and polished, and I brought over a big blue Dutch jug to put on the bookshelves until I can sort out the books, and I put two matching Dutch plates on either side; and I had forgotten a large Wilton carpet that was in the loft, in reds and greens, and that, on the library floor, with the long oak table, made it all look lived-in already. Before the winter sets in I must have—what shall I have?—Some great gathering of people here. Perhaps some great scholar, a philosopher or poet or an astrologer to draw us together and out to wider thinking and deeper understanding of this great and growing world.

Sunday 22nd September

I told everyone after meeting that next Sunday would be a day when I would especially be glad to have them with me to offer the new wing of Moyles Court to God, for His service in and among his people. We would dedicate ourselves and the building to Him, and I needed their support so that it would be used with reverence and generosity. They were sweet. All looking forward to seeing it, and those of our household, who already know it well, after yesterday's hard work, were full of enthusiasm. "We will make sure everyone knows about it and we will all be there", they said.

Ken came to me afterwards and said Joanne very much wanted her parents to come from near Fritham but her father has only one leg (the Dutch war) and—I interrupted him. "Bring them on Saturday in the light waggon, as far as the Ashlys in Linwood, and then bring them all down on Sunday

morning and take your in-laws back after meeting". I was glad
to be able to do that for Ken. He is such a loyal servant and it
is difficult to repay him (except by getting Phyllis off his
hands!).

Monday 23rd September

Went over in the afternoon to make sure all was safe in my
locked chest and that the moving had not disturbed John's
papers. They were in disarray and in tidying them I found
some poetry of Sir John Denham's, and my eye caught this
about the Thames (I'm sure Sir J.D. was writing of the great
Thames of London, but to me it was my little Thames of
Ampney Brook):-

"Thames, the most loved of all the ocean's sons
By his old sire, to his embraces runs;
Hasting to pay his tribute to the sea,
Like mortal life to meet Eternity."

The little drops of mortality that dripped off my fingers
must by now have reached the ocean of Eternity—is that what
happens to us in Eternity, a merging for a new identity? John
H. kept that news sheet for, I suspect, another poem about
the "Progress of Learning"—

"All human wisdom to divine is folly;
This truth the wisest man made melancholy;
Hope, or belief, or guess, gives some relief,
But to be sure we are deceived brings grief."

Yes, that's John H. He sees a truth with clarity, and then,
when he finds it is not the whole truth but only a part, and his
goal (of God) as far away as ever, he loses confidence. Oh,
John, I trust your heart! Oh, let it lead you when your mind
falters!

Tuesday 24th September

This morning's news has made me look back over this year—
turn back the pages of this diary—and marvel at the timing of
things—the orderly sequence—everything in its place, and
events following hard on each other's heels, but always with a
gentle orderliness so that I could live each event, savour each
new meeting and experience, and learn from all that has come
to me.

To-day's news is from son John. Tryphena has left Lloyd and is going to join Bridget in New England, and is staying with them at Dibden until she sails—from Portsmouth on October 2nd. She arrived yesterday and John wrote, not just to tell me, but to ask if I would allow Tryphena to visit me before she leaves. This is, I fear, Bridget's wish more than Tryphena's, but, of course, she must come here. I would be grieved otherwise. I shall invite her here on Monday, 30th, for the night—the day after the dedication of the nw wng—and I shall then be able to give her all my thought and time. At no other moment in the year would I have been so free to devote all my thought and care to her—a short time, but all hers.

Wednesday 25th September

Tryphena at Dibden! Part of me wanted to call Ken and drive over at once. But, no. If I did that she would simply see me as the mother who would not leave her alone. I can hear her child's voice now as she stamped her foot and said, "Go away!", as she pulled butterflies' wings off to 'see how they go!'—and, later, the girl saying, "Oh, mother, leave me alone; I must find out for myself". Until finally she went off with Lloyd—and has found out for herself. She hid away from me and must return to me only if she wishes to. If I go to her it will show disrespect for her individuality, her independence and perhaps, by now, her maturity. I will even use the post and not send my reply by my messenger. I must show loving understanding and God must shower this richly on me and drown my sorrow that we were ever estranged.

Thursday 26th September

Sent my letter to Tryphena. Oh, God, bless it!

Turned my mind to my larger family and preparations for Sunday meeting.

Friday 27th September

In the morning the men moved the benches from the old Chapel over to the new wing for Sunday. The men were a little surprised when I asked Pilbeam to tell them to bring tools—hammers, saws, wood chippings, left-over nails—*any* signs of the work they had done—and arrange them on a carpenter's bench to offer to God the work of their hands. Pilbeam later came and said, "Madam, the farm and stable men want their handiwork blessed too". So they brought a horse-collar and brasses and a bridle, a pitchfork and a bale of corn, and the whole thing caught on, and the window sills became displays of cooking pots and ladles, and things from the dairy, and clothes pegs and a laundry basket, and lace and a lace-pillow with bobbins. I had never thought of anything like this. It looked so vigorous and alive!

Saturday 28th September

In the morning I collected flowers from the garden and arranged them—beech leaves and big white daisies and red and orange dahlias to go in the fireplace. And I brought in the Bible and my copy of Milton and George Herbert and a little leaflet of my own poems and (no-one would recognise this) John H's manuscript from his chest, and put them on the shelf near my flowers—but the Bible on a special table in the front. And I looked round and marvelled. All was expectant and ready. I had no need to ask God's blessing—it was all around me.

Rev. Compton South came in the evening. He was amazed at the display. I had a guest room ready for him. He was to be our first visitor in the new wing, and he said he was "honoured". We spent the evening planning the service for to-morrow when the newness and strangeness will be broken and we must feel a unity and readiness for change and new insight. Solomon's dedication of the Temple seemed to have the spirit we needed. He is going to preach on the text, "Will God indeed dwell on the earth?" and pray Solomon's prayer that "Thy eyes may be open day and night to this house . . .". So I left him. Had his supper sent over. Our first visitor has arrived.

Sunday 29th September

"And it came to pass"—we had our dedication meeting in the morning in the new wing. The hall was very full—everyone seemed to have managed to come—but just before we began, there in the gallery were John, Catherine and Charles, and with them—Tryphena! I could not believe my eyes. I smiled up at them but could do no more to greet them for I was below and hemmed in by crowds. I forced my heart to calm its feverish beating, and disciplined my mind to attend to the purpose of the meeting and give it my full concern. It was hard but I did it.

Rev. Compton South was at his very best and spoke movingly about those who will come within these walls in the years to come, "foreigners and strangers from far-off countries" and "those who go out to do battle", "those who are sick or have sinned", for all who come here, and he prayed that "they may all know that this house is built in Thy Name".* "Hear Thou in this Thy dwelling-place and forgive, and act, and render to each whose heart Thou knowest, according to all his ways, for Thou, Thou only, knowest the hearts of all the children of men". Then he read Solomon's blessing of the people, and then there was a long silence. Before we left he asked us to say to each other as we went out, "May the Lord preserve your going out and coming in", and as we did this many eyes were full of tears—and none more than my own as I met Tryphena.

Monday 30th September

John and Catherine went home yesterday after lunch and, after all our congregation had gone, I said to Tryphena, "Come over the ford with me and we will look for Bridget's oak tree". So began a careful, thoughtful, cautious, even awkward, feeling towards each other of a mother and daughter who had never been close and who had been wrenched apart and out of touch for five years. We are both adult now. We each wanted understanding; each of us had been hurt by the other. Each of us is strong-willed and sensitive. We got through. "I hated you and father being so divided". (And I thought I had shown only loyalty to him.) "You never tried to understand me . . ." "I wished I had been a boy and then you would have let me go". (And I thought she had never been held by me.) "I am a person who must learn by her own experience". (And so am I, and I never allowed her the chances I most needed myself.) Later she told me of Lloyd; she still loves him, but can stand his narrow life no longer. She and Bridget and John have always kept in touch. She said, "I think Bridget needs me now, as I have so often needed her". She said, "Mother, I was deeply moved by old King Solomon's words yesterday", and, "I admire what you have done". My heart sang. This time Tryphena can leave me; this time my spirit will go with her.

OCTOBER

Tuesday 1st October

Tryphena was up early and rode over to see Margaret. She had never before seen little Jenny, of course, and James had been only a baby when she went away. She was back by noon and her boat to-morrow sails on the evening tide—so she did not leave until about 4 o'clock and we had a last few hours together, walking in the gardens, visiting old spots she had remembered when she stayed here as a child. We were relaxed adults together, exchanging experiences and thoughts; she has not a literary or philosophical mind, but is interested in people and relationships—learning the hard way, through Lloyd and, I suppose, me. And so, Ken brought round the little carriage and she went. I went upstairs and saw the carriage fade away through the trees, from the gallery window. Then—down to the new wing. The men and women had removed their treasures, hallowed now and dedicated. Benches had gone back and I threw away the fading flowers, returned John's manuscript and dipped into his Milton before I left.

Wednesday 2nd October

It is dark to-night and no moon or starlight, and somewhere in the Solent will be Tryphena's boat, carrying her away. The daughter who has come closer to me in this last week than she has ever been before, is now, each moment, being carried further away than ever before.

Thursday 3rd October

An empty day. An anti-climax after the last week. Mused on "near" and "far"—how relative, and how meaningless! Those who are really close to me are nearer than those who stand at my side.

Friday 4th October

John's stable boys, Timothy and one I didn't know, rode over from Dibden and brought a note from Catherine and one from Tryphena. Catherine said, "We saw her on her way . . . the boat sailed just as darkness was falling . . . she seemed very torn about going—looking forward to joining Bridget, thankful to have left Wales, but sad, she said, to leave her new-found mother".

Tryphena's note simply said: ·

"Dear Mother,

I am sending you a riddle such as your gandson James would approve:- When I last left you, I had never been near you. This time I leave and will never be parted from you. I think you will understand—
Tryphena."

Saturday 5th October

I have to lead the meeting to-morrow as I received a message from Rev. South that he is in bed with a chesty cough and cold. Perhaps I should not have let him sleep in the new wing so soon. The plaster must still be damp and these autumn evenings are chill. But his bed was well aired and the hangings were thick and it had a new rope base. Perhaps I was too hasty. Winter is coming. But the kitchen ovens and the big fireplace will surely warm it? Planned the meeting around the thought of handiwork—"Prosper Thou our handiwork", for that was the thought left with us after last week . . . the work of hands . . . the miracle of hands . . . for touching, healing, feeling, creating, constructing, serving . . .

Sunday 6th October

Not very many came to meeting. Last week's effort—and effect?—enough for two weeks? But the faithful and regular were there and we were at peace together. I asked them whether they would like us to transfer the conventicle to the hall in the new wing permanently. Very solemn faces and shy comments about "our home", "familiar", etc., and then dear old Harris stood up and said, "We have known many changes in our lives and we live in a time of great restlessness and uncertainty . . . We meet here Sunday by Sunday to find the

139

changeless, eternal Spirit within and among us . . . We would hold our still centre within these dear walls, which for nearly four years have been our security . . ." and he went on a bit, and all eyes were on him, and I heard his message clearly. When he sat down we waited in silence for some time. Then I stood and said, "So be it", and they said, "Amen". So—we stay here. Oddly, and rather surprisingly, I agree with them. I am still a little afraid of that new building.

Monday 7th October

We are well into October and the pigs are out among the acorns and the forest is turning to flame and gold. This month has nothing ahead that I know of to disturb our routine, and I must firmly pick up the reins of authority again and we must prepare for winter. Fruit stored. Nuts gathered. Herbs dried. Pickles, spices, salting. Windows to be sealed with sacking. Straw round the fragile plants. Winter clothing brushed and shaken, and extra covering for the beds. All the *little* things as well as the big ones. I have been offered two men from the Shaftesbury estate—one the ostler's boy who befriended James Dunne, and Roger, a carpenter's apprentice with a permanently twisted knee, so unable to do heavy work. The carpenter one could take over the care of the new wing, and sleep there in the kitchen and be servant to the guests. The ostler's boy, George, could work partly under Harris and make the drive and gardens there good. I knew I would have to have extra staff.

Tuesday 8th October

A letter to-day by post-chaise going to Fordingbridge, from Elizabeth, Countess of Marlborough, to tell me of Thomas Traherne's death—a lovely man and beautiful poet, and I grieve at his passing. She had had Dr. Bowles to stay with her at their London house, and sent me these hints that he had given her:- *For Deafness*: Take four drops of the juice of Betony and warm it in a saucer, then drop two drops in your ear as you go to bed, then stop them close with black wool, and your hearing will recover.

For a cough: Take the syrup of Hyssop and syrup of Licorish, and syrup of Maidenhair—an ounce each—and take a spoonful or two night and morning. (Much like what I used to give the children!)

For headeache: A hand ful of spearmint, shred small, grate nutmeg into it with rosewater, bind it close on your forehead and the pain will go.

These simple country remedies seem far better than the chemicals and pills the apothecaries are too ready to give nowadays. I am interested that even the famous Dr. Bowles— an F.R.C.P.—should recommend them! Must suggest the betony remedy to Althea for her old father. The last potion I gave her has done him no good. (Oil of lavender and rosewater.) I might try a little myself, as I think I *am* a little deaf.

Wednesday 9th October

A day of marvellous autumn colour—the beech leaves bronze and gold and falling as a carpet of rare coins on the forest moss. They were hunting to-day from Fritham and came near the house, and drove two of the fallow deer onto our land and they have been grazing in the wood all evening. Henry Carver brought back a deer that they killed near Ringwood and I went out to see that they hung and salted it for winter. Recollected Andrew Marvell's poem written after he had spent some weeks in the Forest:-

"The wanton troopers riding by
Have shot my fawn, and it will die.
Ungentle men! They cannot thrive
Who kill thee. Thou ne'er didst alive
Them any harm, alas, nor could
Thy death yet do them any good . . .
. . .
It cannot die so, Heaven's King
Keeps register of everything,
And nothing may we use in vain.
E'en beasts must be with justice slain."

There is so much wanton destruction about—such irreverence for living things. The trees are slain for the King's navy, animals for sport as much as food, and greed governs, and lust for possessions. It is fearful when vandalism and thoughtlessness destroy living and lovely things. I, here, am the guardian of great treasures.

Thursday 10th October

Milton:-

"We that are of purer fire
Imitate the Starry Quire
Who in their nightly watchfull Sphears
Lead in swift round the Months and Years.
The Sounds, and Seas with all their finny drove
Now to the Moon in wavering Morrice move."

(Morris dancers came through from Brook to Ringwood to-day, with the mummers, but no plays.)

Orchestra,   Sir John Davies:

"And to the sea, that fleets about the land,
And like a girdle clips her solid waist
Music and measure both doth understand
For his great crystal eye is always cast
Up to the moon and on her fixed fast.
And as she danceth in her pallid sphere
So danceth he about his centre here."

Friday 11th October

Thomas Traherne's funeral is to-day. I thought of him so much. I met him a year or two after the Restoration, at Ted-dington; I remember it was a week or two before I returned to Moyles Court. He had just finished a "Felicity" for Susannah Hopton,* and I still have the paper on which he wrote an extract for me. I took it into the woods (to see if the deer had got safely away) and read it again:-

"Suppose a River or a Drop of Water, an Apple or a Sand, an Ear of Corn or an Herb: God knoweth infinite Excellence in it more than we; He seeth how it relateth to Angels and men; How it proceedeth from the most perfect Lover to the most perfectly Beloved; How it representeth all His Attributes; How it conducteth in its place, by the Best of Means to the Best of Ends: And for this Cause it cannot be Beloved too much. God the Author and God the End is to be Beloved in it. Angels and men are to be Beloved in it. And it is to be highly esteemed for all their sakes. Oh, what a Treasure is every sand when truly understood! Who can love anything that God has made too much? His Infinite

142

Goodness and Wisdom and Power and Glory are in it.
What a world this would be, were everything Beloved as it
ought to be . . ."

We had much understanding together of the reverence and
relatedness of all created things—their coincidental inter-
woven embrace—only recognisable by Love.

Saturday 12th October

N.B. To roast a haunch of Venison after the Best Fashion:

Season it a little, then let it lie a while in warm water; after
which sprig it with Rosemary. Roast it well by a soft fire,
and make for it your sauce with Claret-wine, grated Bread,
Ginger, Cinnamon, Sugar and acid Apple or Currant juice
or lemon juice. Boil them to a thickness of melted Butter,
put it into the dish, lay the Venison on top, and serve.

To make a good Cake:-

Half a peck of Flour, 3 pounds Butter, Nutmeg, Cloves and
Mace, Cinnamon, Ginger and a pound of Sugar. Mix well
with the Flour. Add four pounds of Currants, washed and
picked over and dried, a little Yeast, twelve Eggs, a quart
of Cream or good Milk warmed, half a pint of Sack, a quarter of Rose-water. Knead well, and let it be lith, lay on a
warm cloth, half an hour against the fire, then make it up
with the white of an Egg beaten with a little Butter, Rose-
water and Sugar. Put it in the Oven for one and a half
hours.

(From Elizabeth's letter—she got these from a London
friend.)

Sunday 13th October

Thank goodness, Rev. Compton South is better. He came this
morning, not last night. (I suspect his wife told him not to risk
another night in his new room). I apologised and said I felt to
blame for his cold. He blew his nose loudly and said he was
recovered. I said I would not let him sleep over there again
until all was dried out and warmer.

Meeting seemed like old times—quiet, united, determined.

Rev. C.S. read from two news sheets recently received from London. One was taken from part of John Bunyan's "Pilgrim's Progress", and one from a political pamphlet. He warned us not to expect our social status and standard of living to be improved because our religion was popular with the King. No Declaration of Indulgence by any King (and because of the last one our group is approved) is a step for us up the ladder to prosperity. Acceptance of our status, under God, whether high or low born, is "a sign of our allegiance to the King of Heaven". Bunyan makes Christian say, "A man forward in religion grew acquainted with one 'Save-Self', and then he became a stranger to me". Even, C.S. said, "they jeered at Jesus, saying, 'He saved others, himself he cannot save' ". Hard, yes, but we *must* accept this.*

Monday 14th October

A lovely poem was sent to me to-day by young Thomas Traherne who died last week. I first heard through him of Mrs. Hopton of Kington who runs a group like mine and shares my faith in imaginative freedom. She, unlike me, travelled through Catholicism, back to the Church of England, and was a Royalist with a Parliamentarian officer husband who swung back to the King. I thank God for this turbulence, in faith and politics, so that we who believe in our freedom in God can let our imagination, which is the Spirit of *God* in us, be free to lead us as He will. Here is Thomas Traherne's poem:-

"The Image:

If I be like my God, my King
(Tho' not a Cherubim),
I will not care,
Since all my Pow'rs derived are
From none but Him.
The best of Images shall I
Comprised in me see;
For I can spy
All Angels in the Deity
Like me to ly."

Memories, as so often, of the February fog, and of God within, and eternity the light of this moment, of Now.

Wednesday, 16th October

Walked to Ringwood to-day, through the barley stubble by the farm path* to keep Harriet company. She had geese to drive to market, and honey to sell. They were digging potatoes! (First year here of this new vegetable—memories of roast ones at Bibury Court!). Came back along the river, and swans and geese were feeding on the water meadow and—a swallow, though I thought the last went a week ago. James Dunne caught a salmon and said he would bring it up to Moyles Court to-night. We watched him play it from the bank, and it struggled and lashed and thrashed the silver rushing water. "Must *all* life be an agony?", I wondered, "even for fish?". Came through the woods—beeches all burnished and young oaks browning. We drank ale in Ringwood and had cake with Annie Miller the new apothecary's wife—now a staunch member of Ringwood meeting. She told me of rumours of James, Duke of Monmouth, now in France, and some are wondering whether he might one day come to the throne. John Hicks confidentially had spoken of this to me months back. (He has met him.) I guarded my tongue, for who to-day is friend, who foe, when religion and politics are so interwoven?

Thursday 17th October

Unbelievable news this evening. The night was wild and stormy, and rain fell all day and we heard trees crashing in the Forest. It cleared early in the evening and a watery sun broke through, and just before dark there was shouting and raucous singing in the yard. Harriet hurried in to tell me two drunken sailors from Lymington had come with news of Mr. Hicks! I hurried out to be told they had been given a letter from him to deliver to me, but had fallen in the river at Brockenhurst and it had been lost. They had come to tell me he was in Amsterdam, but they had no idea whether he was coming back to England or what had been written in the letter. They were too drunk to be coherent, too wet and muddy to think of anything I asked them. We gave them dry breeches and some sacking and food, and said they might stay in the stable loft for the night, but they said they would move on to the White Hart

145

in Ringwood where their companions were expecting them. I was not sorry they left, but utterly perplexed about John. What had he told me in that letter?

Friday 18th October

After noon the two drunkards who came last night appeared again, sober now, and dry, but scruffy and very penitent. They had brought part of John's letter which one of them had found in the sleeve of his jacket when they stripped to get dry at the White Hart. Only part of it, and the parchment stuck together and the ink faded and badly smudged. The men were sailors on a Dutch boat bound for Lymington, and had met John on the quay in Amsterdam. He gave them the letter saying if they delivered it safely they would get food and a warm night's lodging. I gave them food and thanked them, and they were decent, honest men to take that trouble. Sailors lost in the Forest are indeed lost! I let Ken take them with the horses to the Naked Man, for from there they can see the Island and the track is clear to Lymington. And so, up to my room to study these tattered remains. All I can really puzzle out is this:-

". . . from Amsterd. . . over two months . . . and the boat was so . . . it was clear it would nev. . . captain made for the . . . Ireland and we were lucky . . . too ashamed to return to . . . Jonah thrown from the belly . . . my passage here . . . many friends. Now I . . . to England . . . this Jonah the people of Nineveh . . . I will come to you . . . may understand what calls me back.'

Saturday 19th October

Oh, John, John! Half your letter is too damaged for me to decipher and I have only the right-hand side of the page that I can even begin to puzzle out! You never reached the New World?—I felt that! You *were* running away? I knew that! And now you know it! Dear Jonah! You are coming back! But *when*? Oh, Jonah, John, when? I think I already understand. I think I knew when you went away in July, and I understood your two wars—the internal war to hold to your spiritual values, and the external war to express these in action in the world.

I think the boat was not seaworthy and they must have made for Ireland and John went from there to Holland—feeling like Jonah, thrown out by the whale, but soon to return to England—his Nineveh?

Sunday 20th October

John had been fading as the weeks passed. Not from my heart—there he is secure for ever. But my clarity of thought about him was fading. Now even a sodden, half-destroyed, blurred letter, wrinkled with water, with words broken and thoughts only guessed at, and the whole a puzzle, brings him close again.

I could say nothing, of course, at our meeting, though I longed to share the news and ask the others to help me puzzle it out. But no, he trusts me, and I would never betray that trust. I tried not to let the sparkle in my heart shine in my eyes. That is something one cannot do! But they never noticed.

Monday 21st October

A quick visit from Margaret and the children who had been to Ringwood with Robert, who had gone to see Rev. South with the latest London news sheets. The children were full of riddles again!—I laughed within me, for no-one knows the riddle I have been trying to solve since my precious half-letter reached me last Friday.

Tuesday 22nd October

Must record yesterday's riddles and hope to remember them, for whenever James comes he asks me them, and I forget the answers!

1. He went to the Wood and he caught it.
   He sat him down and he sought it,
   Because he could not find it,
   Home with him he brought it.

   Answer: A Thorn!

2. What work is it that, the faster you work, the longer it is e'er   you have done, and the slower you work the sooner ye make   an end?

   Answer: a Spit—if you turn is slowly, cooking is quicker!

147

Dear James—he is growing so fast and can now read quite well, with little Jenny struggling to keep up, but much happier among the patterns of autumn leaves and polishing conkers and painting faces on the acorns!

Wednesday 23rd October

John Hicks is *here*, and my heart lays down its load. He arrived in the afternoon, and his letter that was lost in the river was to tell me he was coming back and would I be ready for him unannounced some time this week. Of course I was surprised, but he saw I was so obviously delighted that he never realised until I told him much later that I had only received part of the news of his letter. Took him to see the new wing, and he was impressed, but quiet!—I gave him 'his' room—the one with a private study, which I will keep for him always and he will have his own key. No need to hide his things under the grain any more, now that the old oak chest is in there for him with his cloak and papers. He smiled. "I shall miss the granary", he said. "I felt one with the poor there". "Then be one with them here", I replied, "and pray that they may all, one day, have our freedom and our privileges". "Freedom?" he said—"To come and go, yes, but I feel driven, within, by my longings to set others free, and am myself a captive". More words of his to puzzle over! Oh, the joy to have him here—a bit thinner and paler, but—the same.

Thursday 24th October

John still here, of course. He is still very tired, quiet and obviously glad he can be left in peace. But we sat over a fire in his room till very late, and I want to recall what he told me. Just before he went to university in Dublin, he went to stay with an uncle in Somerset. While he was there, one day he went off on an old cob of his uncle's to visit Glastonbury. There he had an experience that has governed him ever since and, "I have told no-one until to-night", he said. He decided to climb the Tor, so left his horse at the coaching inn and set off over a certain Chalice Hill and then on to a path leading to the old tower at the top of the Tor. "I felt heavier and heavier as I climbed", he said, "all energy seemed drained from me, so that, instead of going straight up as I had intended, I took a spiral trail, feeling strangely impelled, and yet resistant, to a force outside myself. I was awed more than afraid of the pressure. I had left on a gusty March day with the spring in my step and unexpected pleasure in my freedom, but as I climbed, a heavy storm-cloud blew from the west to the Tor top. I was determined to reach the top and yet a power was pushing me away and drawing me aside. Then the storm broke round me in hail, lightning and thunder, and I was drenched."

Friday 25th October

At last it abated a little and he tore himself away, went back to the inn where he had left the cob, and sat by their fire, drying off with a glass of hot ale. When he told the inn-keeper he had been caught in the storm on the Tor, the inn-keeper had said, "That, young man, you will never forget. You were caught by the Earth-Force that shapes your destiny. You will return here in spirit again and again, maybe in the flesh, or you may come back here against your will to die. It has been that way for many before you. You are young, but you will never forget." Somehow, John said, he knew there was a profound truth being revealed to him in that storm. He visited the Old Abbey and went into St. Benedict's church, but far from drawing him, as the Tor had done, it repelled him. He saw it as a sham, pompous, disguised, insincere, and he knew he was called that day to fight for his own vision of truth and freedom, for faith in the Spirit within, for the "Deep that calls to deep" that he had known on the Tor. "All Thy waves have gone over me", he said. He rode back over the rhines and poldens in a daze. "I have told no-one of this but you. It was this I thought of when I studied in Dublin."

Saturday 26th October

He left to-day, but I want to record the end of his story. Something had been lightened for him in telling me, and he left looking stronger and was very much more himself.

"And when I was ordained in Dublin I was feeling for a simpler, more direct truth in response to the Force that had met me that day on the Tor, a force that would direct me without an intermediary". "I have never been to Glastonbury again", he said, "though I have sometimes seen the distant Tor. One day I shall return, but not till my work is finished . . . Does that explain me a little to you, my friend?" "A little", I replied. But, as I think over his story, I know I see him truly through it, and I understand and love him more in the understanding. They say that Joseph of Arimathea went to Glastonbury, and that it is King Arthur's Avalon, and that Christ first appeared in Britain there, but that its spirit is more ancient still. But—who knows these things? What John *did* learn that day was to have faith in the Spirit within him and in his destiny which is in the hands of the Spirit that created and still rules the earth—the true Christ spirit—the Force that turned him from the trodden path, the Life-Force for which he is still striving. Strange. Puzzling. True and important.

Sunday 27th October

John's story of his experience at Glastonbury is of the same quality and level as my experience in the fog early this year, when I 'died' in the bog. "As God converse with God for ever-more". What was made clear to John on the Tor was that, for him, the direct and obvious path will never be his way. He tried, in his ordination, to go the direct way, but he has been turned aside by storms within himself to his service of and concern for the poor, the oppressed, the forgotten people. This is, I think the way he is acting out in life that strange experience.

Strange that he never told me this when he outpoured to me last June. I think he was so concerned then for the vagrant poor, and landless rejects from society, and his sense of the great gulf between rich and poor, that this early experience was too deep-buried then to be relevant. I can feel now, when he preaches to us, how much of his deepest feelings he keeps hidden, and how he dare not openly preach his longing for a classless society, *all* land common land, *all*wealth shared, no status given by ownership of property or inheritance.

Monday 28th October

We have all been indoctrinated; by the Church first (memories of my childhood and of my Father's sincere passing on to us of his belief, moral standards, etc.), and now *just* as surely by Protestants. They tell us, just as dogmatically, what we must no longer believe. Too much 'must', and not enough 'what?'. Sir John tried to reverse what my father had taught me, and indoctrinate me with his doctrine of revolt. Certainly 'revolt' got through to me, and I have turned away from both their pressures. I now have faith in my own insights and the insights of others. I recognise the Christ in us all, however cloudy my seeing too often is, and I am left with a great faith and many uncertainties. Now that I am old enough to have many years to look back on, I can see a sure unfolding pattern for myself, and this makes it possible to see the same taking place in my children and then, more surely, and with love and awe, in John Hicks—that dear, strange mixture of courage and diffidence, of fight and passivity, of sure direction and wavering ways, of independent action and a hunger for support.

Tuesday 29th October

Dreams, visions, insights—these things in some strange way are more revealing of eternal truth and reality than the stuff of our surface living.

I made blackberry conserve and sloe gin to-day, and the house was full of the smell of boiling fruit. I made myself busy, so that the back of my mind could escape and assimilate the experience of that young man climbing Glastonbury Tor and feeling at one with the world of sSpirit and the spirit of the ancient ways. Like sloe gin, that quietly preserves and concentrates the essence of the fruit, so the essence of our deepest experiences is distilled and preserved in myth, symbol and legend, in the drama and ritual of the Church, and, if we will, in our interpretation of the great moments of our lives. How hard and rigid it all becomes when the mind, without the heart, frames dogmas and doctrines and theologies. Too hard (hard like granite) for me!

The children appeared from nowhere to 'help' and lick round the preserving pans and ladles, bless them!

Wednesday 30th October

Recollecting George Herbert's (?) words in connection with yesterday's thoughts:

"To worldly things are—? sharp. To Me are blind."

He knew, and he was young when he died, what I feel after and never quite grasp.

Thursday 31st October

Two very 'ordinary' days of busyness in the house, and evenings reading and sewing. I read, sometimes out loud, and Harriet and the girls mend and make and quarrel over the lace-making stitches. Harriet appears to take in nothing and constantly interrupts—"My lady, excuse me—Annie, Phyllis, Jane, *not* that way!"—and yet it is she who quotes back to me exactly, in the days after, what she had heard me read!

Hallow E'en! The boys hollowed out turnips and cut faces in them, and put candles inside, and stuck them on the gate-posts and shouted: 'Traitors! Traitors! Treason! Ghosts!' Plenty of crazy capering and I watched from the landing window and, as usual, hoped they would keep their lights away from the frugal corn. Heard Pilbeam out there, so knew all was under control, and then it began to drizzle and they disappeared.

NOVEMBER

Friday 1 November

House upheaved doing the floors! Everyone on their hands and knees! I wish we could afford new carpets. They are getting more and more popular, and some of the best are made not far away at Wilton. I saw some beautiful ones brought from Turkey when I was in London. But—our old ones must do, and we have no shortage of beeswax and turpentine! I escaped the bustle and went to visit Betty Smithers at Ibsley, and took her some jars of blackberry and apple conserve. The Salisbury mummers were there and the Morris men on their way to Wimborne from Hale, and crowds had gathered. I couldn't get through to Betty's house, but saw Harry in the crowd and gave him the jars, and he ran in with them. Betty came out to me. "My father was a great Morris man when I was a child", she said, and I realised why she had stayed at home. Stayed to watch a juggler and a fire-eater! Fascinated. But rode home through the fields and back by Ellingham cross.*

Saturday 2nd November

Ten years ago to-day since I heard that Sir John had been shot in Lausanne. That strange marriage which was no marriage, for he gave me nothing, save the children, and they were conceived in pain and humiliation. I was his servant, and willingly so, but more a slave bound by law and not with the courtesy of a caring master to his servant and with generous returns. So I am alone, the head of this much-loved household with its human failings and greatness, its weakness and strength. Sir John was away so much that his death barely disturbed his households. It has altered me. I am alone, but I am growing—in independence and strength. I feel I am free to 'grow up', as the children do. I am free of the stranglehold of church and husband, and yet I am deeply part of each in my

153

dissent. I accept the leadership of Christ, as husband far more than father—a trusting, loving husband, and I his serving, loving wife. I am free to interpret the scriptures with the insight of my own mind and need not, blindly, accept the precepts and added doctrines of the episcopal hierarchy. The priests are men, and each of us is loved as much. Oh, John Hicks, I have learnt much from your courage and thank God for you.

Sunday 3rd November

Ellingham with the household for matins. I looked at them all from my high place at the back in the Moyles Court pew, and watched them, still and silent as they listened to the thundering voice of Mr. Hobson who was saying, "There are amongst us those who would read their Bibles and say, '*This* is the Word of God as *I* interpret it'. They do not seem to know that reading is now common amongst us and the Bible is in our own tongue within reach of us all, but it is not *what* you read, but *how* you interpret that reveals the Word of God. Here the teaching and preaching of the Church, through the Fathers, and the learning and scholarship of the divines up to our present day, can reveal the truth of the Word of God."

He quoted from Bp. Hooker to prove his point, and I knew the solemn bright eyes of my people had no idea of what he was saying. I knew, and in my heart defied him. I *will* be free to 'grow up'. I am loyal to my King, my Church and my God in Christ, and I trust my God to show *me* my way, reveal his truth to *my* mind, and they can dictate and shout and use candles and music and all the symbols of doctrine and art to win me to devotion to *them*, but I am the servant of Christ and God is my Husband—*not* Father, if this makes me for ever a child, never to grow to my own maturity.

Monday 4th November

After evensong last night we walked back and had a late meeting in our meeting house, and I said much of what I wrote yesterday. I came back, sharing Harriet's lantern, and we talked of our group that are faithful in our meetings. She, even she, does not know of my love for Mr. Hicks.

Robert and Margaret drove over from Fordingbridge with

four friends whom I had not met before. We had all been disturbed by the teaching and preaching in the churches that day, and *all* had, and shared, our deep awareness and insight into our own souls' stirrings and recognised our *own* truth. It was beautiful to be with them and feel a serenity and acceptance, instead of the anguish of our passive role and struggle in our pews as the sand slips through the glass. Rev. South says Mr. Hicks may be here next week, and wanted me to know. Raining when they left and mist coming up from the river, but Rev. South and I sat over a new log in the library until late and Harriet brought us warm punch, and sat on a stool at our feet, saying nothing, but dimly aware, I think, that we are *all* servants of one Master, she and I and Mr. South— and Mr. Hobson too, in his pompous way.

Tuesday 5th November

The young people built a huge bonfire this evening and burnt our old tattered scarecrow from the cornfield—said it was 'Guy Fawkes' and in memory of the old Gunpowder Plot! I feared a spark might fall on the barn and in what little hay we have. They were very wild and noisy and excited, and I was afraid and watched from the window. Blazing flames fled streaming as if in terror of their own heat, then writhed and dissolved. Then it began to rain—first a few drops and then a steady downpour, and I saw the flames die down and the dark shapes disappear. They sheltered in the stables from the rain and I sent out gingerbread and cider and hasty pudding and apples and beer. Pilbeam went out and made sure it was safe, and at last all was quiet.

Wednesday 6th November

Robert is much more understandable when he is in company, and especially among men. I really appreciated him on Sunday evening, for he said many things with which I agree. I get angry with him when he is just with Margaret and me, for he is patronising and dour and finds us dull company. I think it is because he knows I disapprove of the way he treats Margaret and she is so sweetly his faithful servant, always looking up to him. That's how the men want their women! How would I have coped with Sir John had he lived to be an old man? He was often away, and that helped, but Margaret has Robert always there, and her only escape is with the children.—But he was different on Sunday and Margaret watched my appreciation of him with such delight.

Thursday 7th November

A long, rather worrying letter from Bridget to-day, though she tells me of Tryphena's safe arrival. But—she is pregnant again. Harvard seems in real trouble, 'languishing and decaying'. Leonard has volunteered a 33% salary cut, and has dismissed their cook and butler and steward. The Old College has been closed and all its valuables are being stored in their house, and there are only four students left. They miss the college routine and the students' cheerful noise, and 'look out sadly on the scaffolding of the unfinished new Harvard Hall which was begun with such joy last August and much merry-making. I watched the building and thought often of your scaffolding on beloved Moyles Court . . . Leonard is very low and speaks often now of tendering his resignation . . . No one seems really to know what has caused all this; Leonard works hard in his own way, but now he has little to do but check the library, list the kitchen and house utensils, and build up a catalogue of Harvard graduates.' It is so sad for them—and Bridget two months' pregnant and surrounded by inhospitable neighbours. Her greatest help is Martha, Biddy's nurse and Bridget's confidante, and of course now Tryphena is there and *should* be a help(?). Her visit here in May and departure in June seem so long ago, and the new wing here now finished and their great Hall hardly begun.

Friday 8th November

A day of heavy mist and chill. Even the oaks are dropping their leaves which fall heavily, damply, and the Forest has a sodden carpet. None of that gay, dancing flurry of the leaves of birch and beech as they flew off in the gusts of last month! The day matches my mood as I re-read Bridget's letter. I can only be sad for both those daughters—so far away and I with so little knowledge of their lives and all that makes up their days. Are there moments of fun and laughter for them? It cannot all be sad? Tryphena won't let it, for she has an unquenchable sense of humour and it will all be so new to her.

Saturday 9th November

Still misty and grey, with dew-covered cobwebs on the shrubs and the flowers in the border. Nearly all colour gone now except for one brave red rose.

Sunday 10th November

Ever since Down Ampney I have been better about Ellingham—in spite of last Sunday's outburst in my diary. I think Bridget Dunch's reverence for the Book of Common Prayer and her understanding of my independent nature, and my sense of relief at being a nobody there and without authority, have given me a humility, badly needed. I *am* a nobody, and too easily and for too long have I seen myself as set above, as *somebody*. This so easily happens to those of us who are by nature non-conformers. That high-up Moyles Court pew doesn't help! But I go there now, not because anyone says I must, but because I *will* to do so. And can keep up the will if Mr. Hobson doesn't attack me, or appear to attack me, or get too pompous, or go on too long!—But to-day was all right, I was able to pray *with* him and through the Prayer Book. I am indeed a drop of living water, but only one small drop in a stream that grows to a great river and then joins the Eternal Ocean.

Wednesday 13th November

I have written nothing for two days. Roger, the new young carpenter, finished the library bookshelves and has done them very well, and is making two lovely carved oak box benches with off-cuts of the seasoned oak left from the panelling, and already half-carved, so all harmonious. I called Phyllis and Katie and the new young Deborah from Godshill to clean through and polish everything. They must learn to work unsupervised, and I must convince Phyllis that she is trustworthy, though I'm not convinced myself! I knew she would flirt with Roger, but I knew that the men, on the whole, have little use for her, and Roger, when he is working, is not easily distracted. It was cold over there and I had a fire lighted to speed the drying out, and I myself filled a shelf with Sir John's old books (the ones my royalist son would not look at, so *that* shelf made me look a real rebel!). Then I brought over some of my own—James Dunne went to and fro, fetching and carrying for me, with a will. I put some of my favourites opposite to Sir John's, so that those who scanned my shelves to find me would be confused and perplexed!

Thursday 14th November

I am no good at moving books for practical purposes like dusting or arranging! I am too quickly distracted and then absorbed. I found a poem in an old collection I had when I was young—I remember it was a favourite that I took with me to the Island when I married—before the Civil War—before I discovered what my husband was really like. I remember thinking he might one day in our marriage enjoy it with me . . . The poem I found yesterday had passed me by then, but now was meaningfull. The poet* speaks of a woman much older than he, and she regrets the age difference:-

> "There are two births, the one when light
> First strikes the new awaken'd sense;
> The other when two souls unite;
> And we must count our life from thence."
>
> . . .
>
> "Love then to us did new souls give,
> And in those souls did plant new pow'rs;
> Since when another life we live,
> The breath we breathe is his, not ours;
> Love makes those young, whom age doth chill,
> And whom he finds young, keeps young still."

Friday 15th November

John Hicks came! John came! He came! Unannounced!—A letter sent ten days ago never arrived (that's why my mind was full of him when I browsed in the books!—he was near at hand!) And the new wing was ready for him, and the fire soon blazing, and the Forest still misty and grey and the days short, and I took him over soon after he had come and showed him his room and his chest and possessions, and he smiled, in a half-amused, half-appreciative way and murmured, "Yes, it is good!", and once or twice again, "It's good!". And I left him with his man to get refreshed and changed, and sent him food and drink, and then soon after dark I went through to him and he was sorting his papers from the chest and had set his things out on the table, and I rejoiced inside and told myself he was settling in and content. We went down to the fire—two good chairs there now—and had *so* much to talk about, so much to share. He is happier, for he seems to be meeting more people who think as he does; in fact, he said, "I am no longer alone".

Saturday 16th November

John says he can stay here until next Wednesday—or at least will be back for nights. He must visit Ringwood, Fordingbridge and Holt, and this morning told me why. I asked him how he slept—"Well and warmly!—I shall always miss my granary—but it was good!" And then he unfolded a plan, with which I was overjoyed to co-operate. He want to bring a group of friends, about ten or twelve, to Moyles Court from November 29th to December 2nd. "We have much to plan and talk over together . . . here we will not be disturbed . . . we can only meet in winter, for we are far apart, when travelling is easier and days are longer . . . will not be found . . . do not all meet often . . . need to strengthen our endeavours, our ideals, our unity." I asked him what binds them together, and his reply was vague—"The plight of our country—the plight of the poor, in body and spirit—the stranglehold of the Church, the power of politics, the barriers between us, and the battles for freedom more often lost than won and, when won, the victory is given to the enemy". "John, for whom do you fight?", I asked. "For the Christ within", he said.

Sunday 17th November

What a different John at meeting to-day!—And everyone surprised to see him. We never expect visitors much between now, with winter setting in, and the beginning of spring—He was so much lighter hearted, and spoke from that bit he loves, about setting prisoners free, and now being the acceptable time. Oh, he is young!—He is still on fire with youthful energy and feels he will set the world to rights with his new gang of similar thinkers. Bless him! He won't do it! But he fires us all with the Spirit—to burn falsehood, to break barriers, to move towards each other in love, to liberate our own deepest selves from the fears and falsehoods which bind us. "Be free!", he said, "First with yourselves, then with each other, then give yourselves in service, to your family, your community, your world, and so learn the perfect freedom of love, and discover within yourselves the Love that is of God". What a fervent "Amen" went up as he finished, and the silence after was long and deep. he went back to Ringwood with the Bolwells, and must have got back very late. I did not hear him come in.

Monday 18th November

John Hicks still here. 'He has the knack of loosening up my heart and I would die for him'. I have heard these words somewhere and take them as mine. He was away soon after breakfast, to Fordingbridge, and back by Holt and here again in the early evening, and we had time for talking and planning his group week-end. They will be entirely on their own in the new wing—with their own servants and preparing their own food! (They are all men and I know what *that* means, so we shall have plenty to do, and I shall call in the extra servants to serve and clear up!). This is why I built the new wing! This is what it is for! New thoughts! New ideas! Entertaining strangers! Open doors and open minds! Some are coming from Plymouth, Kingsbridge and Lyme, and some from Portsmouth and perhaps France—which seems to me unlikely in late November, with fog in the Channel and floods between here and Devon and other hazards. "The only possible time!", John said, "Fog and flood are easier to combat than all the things that separate us when travelling is easier!—at least no highwaymen and robbers!"

Tuesday 19th November

John has recently heard from his brother, Dr. George Hicks, that he has been offered St. Ebbe's church in Oxford early next year. How different those two men are. He told him also that John Milton died of his gout, quietly and with no ceremony, early this month (the 8th). Sad, sad news for England! He was a great and beautiful poet—one I respect more than any other, and one whose thought and philosophy have always influenced John and me profoundly. His Latin prose and poetry are already spreading across Europe, and recognised as great. Also came the shocking news that in repairing part of the Tower of London builders have discovered the bodies of two little children, their arms round each other, buried there. Those two child princes? They think so.

Wednesday 20th November

John has gone again, but will be back in eight days. Portsmouth this time! I have now much to keep me busy. A happy coincidence at noon when Pilbeam came to say that they found two barrels of wine in the cellar! They must be left from my father's days, for Pilbeam said they were clearing out and tidying down there and thought all the barrels were empty for others had been stacked on top and in front. They have had water seeping in down there—left, Pilbeam says, from the wet summer—and the empty barrels were afloat and these two remained stable. They have had a lot of trouble with flood water, but at last they have got it away, cutting a channel through to the stream, mostly under the very old structure down there. Pilbeam had taken Mr. Webb down in August for advice about the damp and smell. Anyway, the problem is more or less solved, and we have two barrels of wine! One I will use for the group week-end! My father's money for the building, and now his wine to celebrate its use!

Thursday 21st November

Only just over a week to get ready for John's group. They had planned to meet in Brockenhurst weeks ago for the night of November 28th, and John is to tell them then where they will be for the week-end. He hoped I would agree they should come here, and probably guessed how proud I would be to have them. I told the household after morning prayers, then to the kitchen to tell them what to prepare, and to the larder to look over the stores, and to the stables to tell Ken what to expect, and—so much to get ready, and lists to make for market next week. Oh, yes, "We will bring our own things, of course", he said, and they will, but I want to add much else for their comfort and pleasure. So preparations began and—it was the collective bustle and activity I so much enjoy, and in the back of my mind the thought, 'This is right, strong, real, for good, for love, for God'.

Saturday 23rd November

Yesterday and to-day spent getting the wing ready except for things that can come over after meeting tomorrow. It looks ready already—all spare stools and benches from the house and even Roger's unfinished benches are able to be used as he has assembled them firmly for the time being. He is such a nice young man and I will let him and George be John's special servants for the week-end.

Sunday 24th November

To-day was not a 'good' day. My prayers come from my head and not my heart; the words were suitable and not sincere. I stayed away from Ellingham as I wanted to make it clear that I am not an Anglican, but oh, to-day of all days, it would have been easy and good to let the Book of Common Prayer do my praying for me, and deceive myself, and let those holy, pious, beautiful phrases speak for me. So I stayed away, and felt worse and not better, and my mind teemed with plans and schemes for next week-end. I am ashamed of myself. I stood out from the whole of our community and was not with them (I think they were unaware—just thought I was having one of my withdrawn, aloof days). The Christian Church should be at one—not all these divisions and distortions and disagreements. But this will never be, till there is neither high nor low, bond nor free, but the sincerity and vision of every individual is seen to be the incarnate God—the Christ—as it was in Jesus. Much penitence, sincerity and tears in my night-time prayers.

Monday 25th November

The preparations began and it was a busy day, sadly interrupted by Phyllis who slipped on the floor she was polishing and broke her leg. Frightened screams came from the new wing and Katie and Roger ran for me, and Harriet and George tried to calm her. She is now strapped to a splint and I gave her a strong sleeping draught. The bone-setter came in the afternoon, and says it should knit straight as she is young and strong. Ken came and said he and Joanne would have her home again, and I agreed, so he and Roger carried her back before dark. "Just as well", said Harriet, "She had started her caperings again and was plaguing poor George, and how many times have I told her to polish with bare feet and not in her ribboned slippers to attract George's attention! . . . It would serve her right if she ended up as lame as George, but the good Lord spares us our deserts and she will be straight enough". Otherwise, all went well with the day.

Tuesday 26th November

I do love this household! Everyone rises to an occasion like this, and it seemed to be busy and happy wherever I went, from stable to wood-shed, to dairy and laundry, coach-house and kitchen. Harriet has brought her young niece, Caroline's youngest, in to help instead of Phyllis. She is only fourteen, but Harriet of course knows her well and will give her work that is suitable, and better a few too many than too few this week.

Wednesday 27th November

To market this morning. I didn't go but sent the cart with Ken and three of the girls and Betty Ashly from Linwood who has agreed to come for the week-end and supervise the new kitchen and the group's servants, and that is a great load off me for she is very reliable and a great friend of Harriet's, and she is so well-known in the market because of her poultry and eggs. We shall be all right, I think, and I am as excited inside as I was as a girl when father expected visitors. I want it to go well, and shall be interested in the men John calls his friends.

Thursday 28th November

We're ready! So much so that, to create composure and peace, I read to the girls in the small parlour and sent the men off for the evening. We all retired early. I went once again to the new wing for a final check, and prayed God that the goings out and comings in there might be blessed, and so to bed.

Friday, 29th November

John and three of his friends arrived just before noon with a waggon full of furniture—not just for their visit but John said, "Will you keep it for me in the new wing?" He had had it stored, for Abigail is very frail and mostly with her mother now, and he said, "This place is home to me". They unloaded it and it fitted well—a desk, a chest, two lovely modern oak chairs, a bed and a virginal. The furniture is beautiful modern oak, the chairs with heavily carved backs and arms. I knew John sang, and have always loved his voice, but had not realised he plays the virginal as well. Everyone was very busy, unpacking and storing, arranging where they should eat, meet, sleep. Two servants came with them, a middle-aged married couple, Edward and Martha Brown, who seem pleasant and capable. My staff helped with the first meal and got it cleared away before dark, just as a group of four more came. I decided I must keep away then, and leave them to settle, and I enjoyed hearing new sounds and voices from different places, and lights in the new wing. John came over late and said, "Madam, thank you for all this. It is everything we want and need". And I was content. There are twelve, counting servants, and two or three more for the day, tomorrow.

Saturday 30th November

Woke to voices and laughter—and remembered! I called to them over the balcony, and they asked if I would join them, with any of my household, for their morning prayers. It was a lovely short, reverent gathering—of few words. John just said, "Let us be thankful" . . . pause . . . "let us be penitent" . . . pause. Then—"honest" "courageous", "dreamers and visionaries"; and then, "Let us act out our insight! Amen". The servants went to their work and John said, "We always have half an hour alone now for our own Bible study. Then we shall return for our first discussion session. Please join us whenever you wish". I was torn as to whether to join them or not, and finally decided to keep away; bury my curiosity, for they would unquestionably be freer without me. It was a right decision. Two of them came just after dark. "We want you with us this evening, Dame Alice! We shall be singing and making music and relaxing". Lovely! So I sent the barrel of wine across and joined them and—puritan?! *Yes*—puritan. Non-conforming puritan! They had a lute and two bass viols, and the virginal, and three good singers, and sang madrigals from Holland and French love-songs, and I got to know the men a little—Hugh, Thomas Everard, Tysoe, Claude (French), Mac (Scottish), Peter Bray; Chris and Bob (Dutch); and two more, I think, who leave early in the morning for Dorchester, and all our servants were there too.

DECEMBER

Sunday 1st December

This is Advent Sunday, and our conventicle was specially good, with John and his group with us and all our local friends and the household. John spoke on 'Coming together', and 'they came to Him from every quarter', and the second coming of Christ and our gathering being a preparation for that. Every coming together, when the common cause and purpose is the love and service of God, is the coming of Christ. The group left quickly afterwards, for their own meeting in the new wing, and we 'locals' were loth to break up and disperse. Only John and Hugh, Thomas and Peter were left by evening, and the nice serving couple who have got on very well with Betty Ashly and Harriet, so that side was smooth-running. I had an hour or so with them round their fire, and we had evening prayers together. I watched their faces as fire and candlelight played on them, all young, John one of the eldest; all vigorous, earnest young men ready to "turn the world upside down". How will they work out the puzzle of their generation? John came back with me to my room. "John, are you looking for religious or political answers to your problems?" I asked. "Can they be separated?" he replied. "Don't worry! We hardly know ourselves yet".

Monday 2nd December

They made an early start; packed the waggon and were away soon after full light. John stayed another hour and left, galloping off to rejoin them somewhere "along the Portsmouth road". He stayed to thank me, gave money to Pilbeam, Ken and Betty and Harriet to share out fairly among the servants. We went over to his room to lock his chest and make sure nothing was forgotten. "A marvellous gathering! A marvellous opportunity!" he said. "What is it all about, John?" "We must find and know ourselves, each other, the Way of God for us, and the Way for the World," he replied. "We cannot lead until we are at peace within and with each other. Too much of our lives has been spent following leaders who have misled, half-truths, half-lights, half-doctrines. We must find and follow the light within each of us, and then let that light lighten the world. This is true leadership—far away from power and pulpit and politics but bringing peace."

Tuesday 3rd December

We cleaned and tidied after he had gone and I left them to get all finished and went to my room and thought long and deeply about all this next generation; Bridget, Leonard, Tryphena, John Lisle, William, Margaret, Robert, Anne, John H., Ken, Hungerford, Bulstrode junior, the young men of this last week-end, all this new generation of my children's age who are now adult, all with their own experiences of life. How different their world from mine! How similar their problems! How different their solutions, when they find them! I thought and prayed for them all and, strangely, for the day of their *deaths*—and my own! That that day which marks the closing of a chapter may be one when each of us may say without shame, "It is finished! Lord, now lettest Thou Thy servant depart in peace!"—No judgment, praise or blame—just peace at the last! Would this sound morbid to a reader? It isn't; it is just looking forward, perhaps a little tiredly, to the end of all this struggling, none of which is of eternal importance, but rather earthily trivial! Peace matters, and Love—nothing else. The essential self of each of us is one with the greater self which is God, the creator and preserver of all mankind. We are all *One*, and that is the truth I have learnt from a lifetime of divisions and parties and strife.

Wednesdays 4th December

How strangely life unfolds! How each piece (day, hour, minute) fits into the whole and makes a pattern as the weaver's shuttle, little by little, reveals design. This year has unfolded a pattern—I look back—though it is not over yet—and see each one of those I love weaving, interweaving, moving as in a dance, toward, away, around, back and forth, dark and light—strange, sure, unity and diversity.

167

Thursday 5th December

Catherine has written from Dibden and asked me to go over from the 16th to the 18th as Edward is coming over from Wootton next week to stay with them until after Christmas, and would like to see me. I am astonished! Is it curiosity about this ageing aunt? Has (and I think this may well be true) Bridget Dunch let it filter through to the Lisles on the Island that I am unlike my husband and need not be shunned by them as Sir John was for his dreadful treatment of his father? Or is something going on about the Crux Easton property?* Or is all this younger generation quietly covering over the family divisions that were caused in our day by the Civil War? It shows my age that I still remember those painful divisions and I am not making allowance for the passing of time. All this is now in the past. I don't want to go to Dibden, but think I must. Perhaps flood or fog, or just plain wet weather, will stop me. Perhaps not. I wish it were my stepson* coming instead of Edward!

Friday 6th December

Harriet and I turned out the spare chest this morning. It must be well over a year since we changed the herbs and lavender and rosemary, and really looked to see what was there. I always do this with Harriet for I am so easily distracted by old books or letters that I never get through, and she won't let me dilly-dally; and she makes me destroy things more ruthlessly than I would myself, and I am sure some things are thrown out that should be kept! I found a litle tea cup and saucer, and a teapot, that I think were given to Margaret when she was a little girl by a naval officer who had been to the Far East. It was wrapped in a lovely piece of apricot-coloured silk which none of us used because we didn't like apricot. I folded it away (Harriet let me!) to keep for Jennie when she is a little bigger. There was a bundle of crumbling letters right at the bottom, from my father to my mother, dated 158-? I could not read a word of it and I wonder if my mother was able to, his writing being so small and full of flourishes. "They were not written for you, my lady", Harriet said, meaning "Throw them away". I didn't, but buried them again right at the bottom.

Saturday 7th December

I had had no fresh air for days, so had a good walk round the estate as, though damp and misty and chill, it was not raining and I enjoyed it. Went to the farm and the barns and the dairy and the two far cottages and called on Joanne and the Ibsley cottages, then up over the moor and back by the Cuckoo pines. Ringwood ringers were practising, and the sound came over in waves and I felt at peace, at home, content. Got back in time to see poor little Polly drop a whole basket of eggs! She was so frightened that she ran off screaming, leaving the basket on the gravel. I went in to Mrs. Bennett to help to make peace. "She won't walk anywhere, but has to run!", Mrs. Bennett moaned. "We all learn this way", I said, and thought how important *all* our mistakes are in life, to help us to learn. Do we learn more from doing wrong than right, I wondered. I don't expect Polly, now aged eight, will do that again!

Sunday 8th December

An interesting couple came over with the Linwood Group; they are staying with the Coopers in Tom's Lane. He is a wheelwright and she a beautiful seamstress. They have just returned from five years in Plymouth, in the new World, where he was a timber feller, and she worked hard making and altering all the ladies' dresses and cutting things down for the children. I hoped for news of New England but they were far away. Jeannie, the wife, was never well, so they have come home. "We're ready to settle down, now", Ted said, and is hoping to be employed as a forester. Pilbeam asked me afterwards if I would pay him to overhaul all our wheels as they badly need it, and we have got carpenters but no local wheelwright since old Smithers died; his apprentice is not yet experienced enough for finer carriage wheels. I approved. We get strangers and travellers coming here and moving on, but not often settling down among us. They are restoring an old cottage that was badly decayed and deserted below High corner, near Broomy Enclosure. People more often move away to the towns than come out here!

Monday 9th December

Harriet and Caroline and Mrs. Hibberd have gone around collecting cloth and furnishings and cookery utensils for Ted and Jeannie. Apparently they have practically nothing in their broken-down cottage. I told Pilbeam to send the waggon up tomorrow with four of our men to give Ted a hand, and fill it with what the women have collected and two chairs and a table and a bedstead that can go from here. Days are short and cold and we must help to get them weather-proof before the worst of the winter at the turn of the year.

Tueslday 10th December

A sad note brought with some newsletters by a messenger who rode straight off, and I never saw him so do not know who he was. The note was from William Lilly, to tell me that the Earl of Clarendon is dying—may by now have died—in France, at Rouen. He was for a short time my friend and he will be mourned by many. It is many years since I heard from William Lilly. (He sent me a copy of his 1675 almanack). There sprang to my mind the idea of asking him here next year—perhaps March or April—to give one of his brilliant lectures on astrology to a group in the new library. I know he gives frequent lectures in London and I know he is both popular and suspect, but for the sake of our old friendship it would be good to hear him. There is so much interest and confusion about astrology and portents and dreams, and he is a great scholar of the influence of the stars, not only over each of us as individuals but over the movement of world forces. I *know* the stars influence my life and form my character. I know some confluence of stars accounts for my relationship with John Hicks and our lives and deaths are strangely linked. And I recognise the Pisces in him so markedly. And I know my dreams have deeper meaning than I can often fathom.

Wednesday 11th December

Wrote to William Lilly. I put the idea to him of his visiting here, as the thought grew in me and seemed good. If he does not come I might find a member of the new Royal Society, which is becoming increasingly influential as a meeting place of all types of new scientific thought. Many of my old friends of the 1630's and 40's are turning up these days. How light-hearted and carefree I was as a young woman, when Elizabeth and Frances Hyde and William Lilly and Bulstrode and I tried to divine with hazel rods and William said I was somehow responsible for the eclipse on May 22nd to 24th 1639, because it was near my birthday! I remember my alarm!—Then all that lighthearted gaiety subsided as I played the role of Sir John's wife and became silent and withdrawn as my views were so opposed to his. Neither Edward Hyde nor Bulstrode could have recognised me then, and what poles apart from each other those two grew (stepson William got to know Edward well when they were both in France with the King—before the Restoration and Edward's earldom and William's knighthood).* I'm reminded yet again of the changes there have been in this century—changes in each of us as well as in society.

Thursday 12th December

A letter from Tryphena. A warm, open letter, telling me so much. Bridget's pregnancy goes ahead and she is, physically, reasonably well, but—"Oh, that man of hers!", Tryphena writes, "scholarly, stuffy, depressed and boring! If he were pregnant one would forgive his moods, but I can't think he will ever give birth to a university as he is now, and things are very difficult". . . . "A strange, rough country. . . We play at being in England on a stage with the wrong background, and sometimes we forget we are in a New World, and then it forces itself upon us, with an Indian problem, or a health problem, or strange food or shortage. It is both exhilarating and alarming . . . Leonard shuts himself in Harvard Library with his books . . . I've met some very nice people . . . We women hang together, working hard, gossiping, keeping going . . . I wish they were less strictly Puritan, although many drink and wench and brawl as much as anywhere else, but with dire punishments for being found out . . . there are real saints and holy people here—struggling to lead good lives . . . You seem so far, far away, dear new-found Mama". Much more, and I read and re-read it.

Friday 13th December

Thoughts still in the new World with my daughters. Tryphena tells me, in a few words, more than Bridget has ever told. Before Bridget came home I had no idea her life was so full of problems. Oh, yes, problems of New England, but not the far deeper and closer ones of Leonard's temperament. Thank God Tryphena is with her, and thank God, too, for my closeness now to that dear daughter from whom I was so estranged—so unnecessarily estranged. I took out of my chest her note to me of October 4th—a precious note (tear-stained, I noticed). This year has had some very special healing happenings—Bulstrode in March, Bridget in early September, Tryphena in October. A year of many blessings— And what a week for letters!

Sunday 15th December

Stupid of me to have agreed to go to Dibden. The forest tracks will be muddy and slippery, and it will be slow going. But I so much want to heal the rifts in the family and this seems to be a year when it is my role to reach out to others in understanding. I suppose I shall always feel alone, different, and misunderstood and misinterpreted. I never get really close to anyone (except for one person), and my struggle to be loyal to Sir John through those thirty and more years of marriage sent my own thoughts deep inside, and only in the last ten years have I been free to be true to myself. So—I set off for Dibden tomorrow, with Tryphena's letter which gives me faith that healing of old wounds *can* take place, where estrangement (especially when caused by stupid things like politics and theological wranglings and dogmas) has built barriers. "With God converse with God for evermore". Must try hard to live the truths I know. Meeting to-day. Rev. Crofts in one of his heavy moods, and he is never interested in me, but he spoke on, 'You are the Christ', and our thinking on this—of the Christ in each of us—was a good stepping-stone towards Dibden for me.

Monday 16th December

I went over to Dibden in mist and heavy rain, stopping for lunch at the new coaching inn at Lyndhurst. They had a huge log fire which was most welcome, and venison turning on the spit. A cheerful party of young men on their way to Lymington were there before us—sailors joining their ship, who had come down with friends from Salisbury on borrowed horses which they could not ride—and their banter was about the 'starboard side of the horse' and 'a man overboard in the ditch', and much I missed!—Ken disgusted by their ignorance and mishandling of the horses. So, on again in the rain, and arrived before dark. Edward really did seem pleased to see me, and has brought over with him his aunt Jane, my husband's and his father's sister-in-law, Samuel's wife, whom I had never met, who lives in an old Lisle property at Crux Easton. He had with him also a crippled French man, Pierre, whom William had brought to Wootton from France as companion to Edward when they came back with the King at the Restoration. Edward wants him to become tutor to Charles as he feels responsible for the man since his paralysis after a riding accident four years ago at Wootton. He has to be carried everywhere in a sedan chair, but is a pleasant and courageous man who could do the job of tutor if John and Catherine can manage it.

Tuesday 17th December

It is turning really cold and wintry, and I was foolish to come away at this time of the year. We spent the day indoors though the men went out to shoot duck. Pierre enjoys hawking and they took him with them. We stayed in Catherine's parlour and talked of tapestry and modern portrait painters and the miniature portraits that are so popular just now. I like Aunt Jane very much and have invited her to Moyles Court for Christmas. I was right to think that the news of my visit to Down Ampney had reached Wootton. "Bridget does much to keep the family together", Jane said, and I felt glad I had asked her to Moyles Court, and think Catherine is glad too. It is not easy to have such an unwieldy household—from grandmothers and great-aunts to children—and the Croke side of the family live near enough to drop in often. Edward seems keen to visit Crux Easton. He talks of leaving the Island and re-establishing Lisles there.

Wednesday 18th December

Left early in the morning. However stupid to travel in December, it has been worth it. I saw little of John, but he seemed glad I had heard from Tryphena and glad I have asked Jane to stay. She has agreed to come from 23rd to 27th. Edward will come, with or without Pierre, on the 26th, and go on to Crux Easton next day. It seems a bit silly to do all this travelling at this time of the year, but perhaps I think that, because I am a little afraid they might get snowed in and be here until next March!

Thursday 19th December

Felt tired to-day, and a bit irritable. I know why. My morning's peace has been disrupted while at Dibden and I easily get upset and disorientated when I miss my hour around dawn for thoughts and prayers and quiet return to my deeper self. I only paid brief visits to kitchen, dairy, stables, farms. They like me to greet them on my return, so that they can re-establish their place in the community and relationships with me. I know very well that things are rather different when I am away. More lenient? More harsh? I am not sure. Perhaps it is only I who want to re-establish my control? Whatever it is, all seemed busy and content, and no-one had any major trouble to report—except coughs and colds and a sprained thumb, and rumours of plague in Ringwood and smallpox at Downton, but no-one is travelling about much so it may only be rumour or, if a small outbreak, it may be confined.

Friday 20th December

What I most needed came about to-day—a package delivered from Portsmouth from John Hicks. He has sent me, in his own writing, some extracts from an old fourteenth century manuscript, never yet printed, which has come his way, and he has sent a long letter too about the group's meeting here, and says, "You were Martha and Mary to us", and . . . "I think you will understand the enclosed which says that, far above your active love for me (the Martha in you), and beyond your contemplative love for God (the Mary), is set 'that high cloud of unknowing' beyond, which is the 'sovereign wisdom of the Godhead' . . . As I read this manuscript I thought of you and wished we could read it together. It speaks of silences we have known and in which we have learnt so much." Oh, John, I needed this to-day! Only yesterday I wrote of my restlessness and lost stillness. It will return. There is a little packet also enclosed which says, "For Christmas. J.H."

Saturday 21st December

Reading John's extracts from 'The Cloud of Unknowing'—deep, beautiful. Needs re-reading and re-reading. He had only sent me short passages and—how can I get in touch with the whole? How did he come across the manuscript? Probably through his brother George? The unknown author says that however high we may go, however far we may travel in the life of the spirit, we are yet far, far from God, but if we faithfully reach out then we pass into the 'cloud of unknowing', the 'divine dark', surpassing reason and beyond words, reaching towards the 'incomprehensive and inexpressible God'. Strange. True. Right. I have dwelt much on the Immanence of God. To be drawn into thoughts of His Transcendence is awesome, humbling, profound.

Sunday 22nd December

No writing. Much thought given to these chapters (17–21) of the Cloud. I would like to have shared it with our meeting, but—it is too difficult and *must* be read and pondered slowly and prayerfully and quietly.

Monday 23rd December

In spite of the peace I have found in my readings, I was driven mad this morning. They were going down from Broomy Lodge to help decorate Ellingham church, and called in. Elizabeth brought me an old oak log, painted up with gold leaf, and I wanted to *scream*. The Forest is God's gift to us and needs no embellishment. Neither does His church, nor His altar, nor His priests. They can't understand me and I can't explain. I scream in silence deep down within me.

175

"It was so beautifully done", they said,
Each beech leaf dipped in gold.
Each Spanish chestnut, holly leaf or frond
Gilded the same and 'tastefully arranged'
In chinks of gilded bark.
All gilded, gilded—'beautifully done'.
'A flower arrangement for the Christmas feast'
—But—feast commercialised, a tawdry rape!
For they held once an autumn glory
As the sun shot golden through the branches
To the forest bed,
On bronzed damp bracken frond and fallen beech
Gilded by the sun's long rays aslant the moss,
The rotten bark, the stone, not to be caught
By golden paint but caught in memory only
Till, covered over by the drift of snow,
And crystallised as for some heavenly feast,
They lie preserved for ever, in the heart—
Most beautifully done.'

Jane arrived just before dark.

Tuesday 24th December

Marvellous day of bustle and activity! Pots in the kitchen bubbling, and the boys turning the spit and burning their fingers; and beatings and poundings of herbs and sweetmeats; and holly and pine and ivy brought from the forest, and everyone who passed broke off branches and brought them in for mantel and shelf and—all felt *good*, *human*, *happy*!—And dear Harriet, of course, everywhere, giving hot punch to the foresters and warm cake and candy to the children, and scolding them for scuffing the fresh straw with their muddy boots and making them walk barefoot in the house! And the men laughing at her, and I, turning away from the men's bawdy talk and stuffing boar's head and turkey and—pretending ignorance, innocence and deafness!—And dear Jane, bewildered but all right. We're having the Christmas dinner in the new library—another chance to celebrate there.

A strange gypsy came just before dark with a great bunch of mistletoe from Dorset orchards. I refused it for its old Druid symbolism, but saw they had hung some over the stable door.

We don't often get any here. Pies and mincemeat after dark, and little by little the folk disappeared—to revelry in Ringwood, I guess, and I saw Aunt Jane to bed and then collected my gifts for the household and members of our meeting tomorrow—braids and ribbons and spices, toffee apples and gingerbread, new pattens for Harriet, and butter and honey and cheeses, and bags of lavender.

Wednesday 25th December

Before dawn I went on to the balcony of the new wing, lighted my candle and opened John's Christmas note. It was a beautifully printed card of a poem called 'Peace', by Henry Vaughan, and he had wrapped it in a paper on which he had written, "He also wrote, 'Certain Divine Rays break out of a soul in adversity, like sparks of fire out of the afflicted flint'. God bless your day. J.H."

—And the day *was* blessed! What a feasting! Capons and ducks and turkey and boar's head dressed with rosemary and bay and spiced with wine and apple, and brawn and pies and puddings with plums and dried fruits, and oranges and violets and rose-petals crystallised in sugar. It was unusual to Jane to find we all feasted together—even the children came in, and the library looked lovely with a huge Yule log blazing and the brass chestnut-roaster that reminded me of my childhood, being refilled over and over by James Dunne (who burnt his arm and much enjoyed my fussing over him). We had music in the evening and singing and our own men made a good Morris Dance team with the older boys and the Rockford Green folk. I gave my gifts and all seemed happy, though Phyllis was sulking and Harriet exhausted. I think Jane has had a happy Christmas, though she knew no-one so it must have been tiring for her. Very cold, frosty night.

Thursday 26th December

A day of clearing up and cleaning. The kitchen staff having time off as we had plenty of Christmas fare. I gave the day to Jane and we had a quiet morning in the parlour talking. She is interested in everyone. "Your Harriet is a treasure!", she said. We went over to Broomy Lodge in the afternoon. (Hannah and Elizabeth had asked us on Monday.) Only a short visit, as much to show Jane our part of the Forest as to see the family. It is cold and frosty, and the sky getting overcast and a feel of snow in the air. Edward arrived within an hour of our return, having had a good Christmas. He has left Pierre to give John and Catherine a chance to see if they can manage, and for Pierre to get to know young Charles. "Aunt Jane has enjoyed her visit!", he said as we parted for the night. I'm glad.

Friday 27th December

John Donne—Sermon, Christmas Day 1624: 'The air is not so full of Moats, of Atomes, as the Church is of Mercies; and, as we can suck in no part of Aire, but we take in those Moats, those Atomes, so here in the Congregation we cannot suck in a word from the preacher, we cannot speak, we cannot sigh a prayer to God, but that that whole breath and air is made of mercy.'

Edward set off with Aunt Jane by mid-morning for Crux Easton, spending to-night near Salisbury with distant Hungerford cousins, and I got ready to go to the Whitakers to-morrow for the night. We have cancelled our Sunday meeting this week.

Saturday 28th December

Went over to Fordingbridge and had a warm welcome from the family. They have had a happy Christmas, but I think their community is more sober and solemn than ours!

Sunday 29th December

Went to Robert's meeting, where I knew very few people and was given honour as "Dame Alice Lisle of Moyles Court", and felt suspect as Sir John's widow, with curious stares around me!—Margaret was sweet, timid and self-effacing, and Robert clearly in command. But it was quite a large group (twenty?) which in this winter cold—snow flurry in the morning—was good, and it was natural, I suppose, that I could not quickly feel at home. The highlight of the day was after we had had a good meal and young James, with a borrowed Cavalier hat with feathers, invited us to 'A Mummer's Play on the pageant in the barn', and little Jenny blew a trumpet to summon us! Margaret and I, wrapped in furs and rugs, sat on bales of hay, and our two, with four little friends, did the George play on the cart with much killing and dragging about of bodies, and a horse that broke in two when front legs capered off leaving back legs on the floor, and all ended with little Jenny being led in by "Joseph" and finding, to her surprise, "my baby dolly in a manger", which James had hidden for her. "It's Jesus!", he whispered to her. "It's Jesus!", she said to us proudly, and we were glad Robert was not there, having to cope with blasphemy and idolatory which mothers and grandmothers can overlook!

Monday 30th December

Home again as powdery snow fell, and I was glad to be back, Moyles Court being warmer and cosier than the Whitaker home. I only got that visit in just in time, for there were heavy grey snow-clouds about and a few snow flurries. I would not be surprised if I wake to a white world. A year coming to an end! What a year! Full and important! Much in it to thank God for, and many in it to commend to His loving care.

Tuesday 31st December

As I suspected, thick snow. How quiet the world goes when the snow falls. There were footmarks in the yard, and the sound of scraping as they cleared a path to the stables and the cowsheds. But the front of the house, as I looked over to the forest, held the silence I love, unbroken and deep, with a slight stir of life as a bird dislodged the snow on a branch and it dropped quietly below. I shared the silence for a long time into the morning.

Next year I am going to start a different sort of journal that is going to have a special meditation or thought for every day of the year. It may take me the rest of my life to complete. I cannot be sure each day that I will have a thought worthy of recording, but—when they do "come"—like butter in the churn, they give me joy and I recognise that they come to me from—? Above?—Outside?—Beyond?—To me and not of me. And to reach out for them each day is my resolution for the New Year. "Behold, I make all things new".

CONCLUSION

So, for Dame Alice, the year 1674 came to an end. Eleven years later, the Duke of Monmouth had failed in his ill-organised and misguided attempt to seize the crown, and had been defeated at the Battle of Sedgemoor. John Hicks, a refugee from that battle, with a young friend, Richard Nelthorpe, reached Moyles Court, and thankfully, no doubt, found shelter with his old friend, Dame Alice Lisle. That night, soldiers surrounded the house and found the fugitives hidden there. They were taken prisoner together with Dame Alice, to be tried for treason. John Hicks was taken from Salisbury to Glastonbury, that place of his strange youthful experience, recorded by Dame Alice in her diary. There he was hung drawn and quartered. Dame Alice was tried by Judge Jeffreys in Winchester, condemned by the jury and sentenced to death.

Voice of Judge Jeffreys:- "I think in my conscience the evidence was as full and plain as could be, and if I had been among you and she had been my own mother I should have found her guilty. So—I pronounce—that you, Mrs. Lisle, be conveyed from hence to the place from whence you came, and from thence you are to be drawn on a hurdle to the place of execution, where your body is to be burned alive till you be dead. And the Lord have mercy on your soul!"

Thus was Dame Alice condemned for treason, the order for burning was deferred for four days and then changed by King James II to execution. The sentence was carried out on September 2nd 1685 in the market place at Winchester.

How can you, who have now come to know Dame Alice so well through her diary of eleven years before, believe that she could ever have been guilty of treason?

NOTES

1 Jan.   This grate is still in the library at Moyles court with 1674 on the back and the rivets confirmed as of 17th century design.

1 Jan.   Sir John Lisle was one of those responsible for the drawing up of the death warrant for Charles I. He was an ardent Cromwellian. Murdered in Lausanne 1664 and buried there.

1 Jan.   Moyles Court Conventicle was started in 1672.

2 Jan.   Aconites still grow in the woods at Moyles Court, but many were buried under Wing House when it was built in 1974.

6 Jan.   Robert Whitaker, dissenting minister at Fording-bridge. Married Margaret, daughter of John and Alice Lisle.

7 Jan.   A "simple" boy who finally became a baker at Warminster and was responsible for directing John Hicks and Richard Nelthorpe from Horton to Moyles Court, and so to their arrest, after the Battle of Sedgemoor in 1685.

13 Jan.   The foundations and lower brickwork were found in 1974 when a new house was built and in digging the footings it was found that the same siting had been chosen as Dame Alice had used. Hence the name "Wing House" for the new building.

14 Jan.   When a refugee from Sedgemoor in 1685 John Hicks was found in hiding in Moyles Court by Judge Jeffreys' soldiers and was therefore the cause of the arrest of Alice Lisle as a traitor to the King.

24 Jan.   Colonel Penruddock was the local Justice of the Peace and the courts were held at Hale House. His father had been brought to trial by Sir John Lisle and there was therefore estrangement between Hale House and Moyles Court as a result.

25 Jan.	Barter was in the district in 1685 and was responsible for telling Judge Jeffreys' soldiers that refugees from Sedgemoor were at Moyles Court. So he was avenged for Dame Alice's action after this theft.
25 Jan.	The pinafore still exists (1985). It was given by the Mist family in 1962 to the Vicar of Ellingham, to be given to Moyles Court—not to the owners—and it was hung, framed, in the library, by the purchasers in 1963 to be part of the house for ever.
14 Feb.	Bridget Hoar, daughter of Sir John and Lady Alice, married to Leonard Hoar, Principal of Harvard University.
27 Feb.	Sir Bulstrode Whitelocke, a great politician and one time Ambassador to Sweden, and Keeper of the Great Seal.
9 Mar.	The Lisle family came from the Isle of Wight and after her marriage Alice Lisle lived at Wootton with her husband.
15 Mar.	Ann Clifford of Wilton House, Salisbury.
17 Mar.	Rev. John Crofts—Private Chaplain to Dame Alice.
22 Mar.	Catherine Croke married John Lisle, son of Sir John and Lady Lisle.
27 Mar.	The Hungerfords were related to the Lisles by the marriage of Bridget Hungerford to Sir William Lisle of Wootton, Isle of Wight. Alice's husband was their eldest son.
31 Mar.	George Hicks, younger brother of John. Tutor at Lincoln College, Oxford; later Vicar of St. Ebbe's, Oxford, and in 1683 Dean of Worcester.

4 Apl.	Catherine inherited the manor of Dibden on the death of her father and she and her husband lived there. The Lisle tomb can be seen in Dibden church.
6 Apl.	Philip Webb, cousin of John Webb, a well-known architect; both were related to and trained under Inigo Jones.
9 Apl.	Alice Lisle inherited Moyles Court from her father, Sir White Beconshaw, on his death in 1662.
13 Apl.	Dame Alice has a karmic premonition of the linking of her life and, as it proved in 1685, her death, with John Hicks. For no-one else would she have given her life so willingly.
14 Apl.	The truth of this was proved when Dame Alice was betrayed by Barter in 1685.
17 Apl.	See note for 13 Apl.
24 Apl.	Leonard Hoar had lived in Boston from boyhood, but came to university in England, returning with Bridget in 1672 and being made, soon after his return, Principal of Harvard University founded thirty years before.
2 May	At the trial of Dame Alice, James Dunne was called as a witness and became impossibly confused when called by Judge Jeffreys for cross-examination. "I am quite cluttered out of my senses. I do not know what I say!" he answers despairingly.
6 May	Sir John Lisle was Warden of St. Cross Hospital from 1643 to 1649. He had lodgings there and also in the Cathedral Close.
8 May	Harvard University was at its lowest ebb from 1673 to 1677 and only just survived closure.
14 May	Tryphena was the third daughter of Sir John and Lady Alice.

20 May	Hezekiah Usher became Bridget's second husband after Leonard's death in 1675.
24 May	A massive oak tree now grows by the ford, reputed to be fully three hundred years old.
27 June	Another example of Dame Alice's premonition of the future and her destiny.
30 June	Leonard Hoar resigned in 1675 and died in November of that year.
12 Jul.	Grinling Gibbons, or possibly a pupil of his, worked at about this time in Ellingham Church.
18 Jul.	1674 is on record as the wettest year since records began.
3 Aug.	Sir John Lisle, Alice's son (first, Beconshaw, died in infancy), was a staunch Royalist. Married Catherine Croke of Dibden and lived there. He never got on well with either parent, being politically and religiously opposed to them, and further divided from them by the Civil War.
5 Aug.	This Bridget was described in 1632, when she ran away, as "a rude girl and ill brought up, her parents letting her have her way in all things".
15 Aug.	Of interest to Catherine, for the Crokes who visited Chilton Foliat on 22 March were her cousins and uncles.
23 Aug.	William, Alice's stepson, was the son of Sir John Lisle and his first wife—Hobart, whom he married for her money. She died in childbirth a year after her marriage.

2 Sep.   The Wilton estate was managed by William, Sixth
          Earl and a bachelor. This younger Anne Clifford
          was a distant cousin of Anne Clifford, Countess of
          Pembroke, and lived at Wilton to act as hostess.

29 Sep.   His prayer embraced those men who set off from
          Ibsley Airfield to fight in the Battle of Britain,
          when Spitfires were hidden in the wood and Moyles
          Court was the officers' mess. Wing House had been
          demolished many years before.

11 Oct.   Susannah Hopton ran a conventicle at Kington
          near Hereford, from which county Thomas
          Traherne came.

13 Oct.   Was Lady Alice trying to come to terms with this
          when they recorded at her trial that she fell asleep?

16 Oct.   These fields are now under water created by the
          gravel extractions of this century.

25 Oct.   In 1685 John Hicks was taken to Glastonbury after
          his capture at Moyles Court, and was hung, drawn
          and quartered there.

1 Nov.   See October 16th.

14 Nov.   William Cartwright, 1611–1643.

5 Dec.   The lands of Crux Easton had been in the Lisle
          family for many generations, but had passed into
          the ownership of the Duke of Albemarle at the
          Restoration. Jane "Lisle", however, still lived
          there, and in 1692 Edward retired there from the
          Isle of Wight and became a keen agriculturalist.
          See also Aug. 23.

11 Dec.   See August 23.

187

12 May Found in London   Beaumont and Fletcher (1610)

London to thee I do present the merry month of May;
Let each true subject be content to hear me what I say:
With gilded staff and crossed scarf, the Maylord here I stand.
Rejoice, O English hearts: Rejoice! Rejoice! O lovers dear!
Rejoice, O city, country, town! Rejoice eke er'ry shire:
For now the fragrant flowers do spring and sprout in seemly
    sort.
The little birds do sit and sing, the lambs do make fine sport:
And now the birchen-tree doth bud, that makes the school
    boy cry;
The morris rings, while hobby-horse doth foot it feateously;
The lords and ladies now abroad, for their desport and play,
Do kiss sometimes upon the grass and sometimes in the hay:
Now butter with a leaf of sage is good to purge the blood;
Fly Venus and phlebotomy, for they are neither good;
Now little fish on tender stone begin to cast their bellies,
And sluggish snails, that erst were mew'd, do creep out of
    their shellies;
The rumbling rivers now do warm for little boys to paddle.
The sturdy steed now goes to grass, and up they hang his
    saddle;
The heavy hart, the bellowing buck, the rascal and the
    pricket,
Are now among the yeoman's peas, and leave the fearful
    thicket.
And be like them, O you, I say, of this same noble town,
And lift aloft your velvet heads, and slipping off your gown,
With bells on legs, with napkins clean unto your shoulders
    tied
With scarves and garters as you please, and "Hey, for our
    town!" cried.
But let it ne'er be said for shame, the we the youths of
    London,
Lay thumming of our caps at home and left our customs
    undone.
Up then, I say, both young and old, both man and maid
    a-maying
With drums and guns that bounce along and merry tabor
    playing.
Which to prolong, God save our King, and send our country
    peace,
And root out treason from the land!
                   And so, my friends, I cease!

"In the beginning of time the great creator, Reason, made the earth to be a common treasury, to preserve beasts, birds, fishes, and man the lord that was to govern this creation . . . Not one word was spoken in the beginning that one branch of mankind should rise above another . . . but . . . selfish imaginations . . . did set up one man to teach and rule over another. Thereby . . . man was brought into bondage, and became a greater slave to such of his own kind than the beasts of the field were to him, . . . The earth was hedged into enclosures by the teachers and rulers, and others were made slaves. And that earth, that is within this creation made a common storehouse for all, is bought and sold and kept in the hands of a few, whereby the great creator is mightily dishonoured, as if he were a respecter of persons, delighting in the comfortable livelihood of some, and rejoicing in the miserable poverty and straits of others.

From the beginning it was not so.

. . . True freedom lies in the free enjoyment of the earth."

July 17th
John Hicks' cutting from the "Moderate"—an article by Gerrard Winstanley, Digger 1647. Found among his papers.

BIBLIOGRAPHY

England in the Seventeenth Century—Maurice Ashley.
English Religious Dissent—Erik Routley.
English Social History—G. M. Trevelyan.
Illustrated English Social History Vol. II—G. M. Trevelyan.
Restoration England—Patrick Morran.
Change and Continuity in Seventeenth Century England—Christopher Hill.
The Century of Revolution—Christopher Hill.
The World Turned Upside Down—Christoper Hill.
Who's Who in History—Christopher Hill.
The Tower of London—A. L. Rowse.
Covent Garden—M. C. Borer.
Civilisation—Kenneth Clark.
The Western Rising—Chevenix Trench.
The Escpe of Charles II—Ollard.
The Protestant Duke—Violet Wyndham.
The Golden Century—Maurice Ashley.
The Later Stuarts Vol. II—Clark.
This War Without an Enemy—Ollard.
The Monmouth Episode—Little.
The Diary of Samuel Pepys.
Pepys and The Revolution—Arthur Bryant.
Penny Merriments—Samuel Pepys.
Proud Northern Lady—Martin Holmes.
The Improbable Puritan—Ruth Spalding.
Pepys Himself—C. S. Emden.
The Man in The Making—Arthur Bryant.
Lord Chancellor Jeffreys and The Stuart Cause—Keeton.
Milton The Puritan—Rowse.
Country and Court—J. R. Jones.
The Pilgrim Fathers—L. W. Cowie.
History of The Berkeley Company—Gethyn Jones.
Harvard in The Seventeenth Century—Morison.
The Mayflower—Kate Caffrey.
Everyday Life in Colonial America—Louis Wright.
The Elizabethan America—A. L. Rowse.
History of New England—John Winthrop.
A History of Hampshire—B. Carpenter-Turner.

Milford-On-Sea Record Society.
Victoria County History of Hampshire—Keppel.
Ringwood, The Monmouth Rebellion—Keppel.
The Bloody Assize—Keppel.